W9-BZC-316

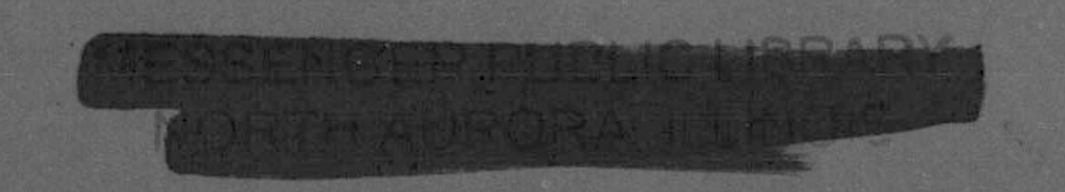
MESSENGER PUBLIC LIBRARY
NORTH AURORA, ILLINOIS

GREAT *party* FONDUES

PEGGY FALLON

PHOTOGRAPHY BY ALEXANDRA GRABLEWSKI

JOHN WILEY & SONS, INC.

This book is printed on acid-free paper.

Published by John Wiley & Sons, Inc., Hoboken, New Jersey
Published simultaneously in Canada

For general information on our other products and services or for technical support, please contact our Customer Care Department within the United States at (800) 762-2974, outside the United States at (317) 572-3993 or fax (317) 572-4002.

Wiley also publishes its books in a variety of electronic formats. Some content that appears in print may not be available in electronic books. For more information about Wiley products, visit our web site at www.wiley.com.

Book design by Elizabeth Van Itallie
Food styling by Brian Preston-Campbell
Prop styling by Barb Fritz

Library of Congress Cataloging-in-Publication Data:

Fallon, Peggy.
Great party fondues / Peggy Fallon ; photography by Alexandra Grablewski.
p. cm.
Includes index.
ISBN 978-0-470-23979-7 (cloth : alk. paper)
1. Fondue. I. Title.
TX825.F22 2008
641.8'1--dc22
2008009575

Printed in China
10 9 8 7 6 5 4 3 2 1

FOR ADAM, JON, AND DAVID —THE NEXT BEST THING.

"In a country where people eat fondue, there can be no wars."
—Anonymous

CONTENTS

ACKNOWLEDGMENTS

Many thanks to Justin Schwartz, senior editor at John Wiley & Sons, who believed in this project from the very beginning.

My sincere gratitude to Linda Gollober and Ann Tonai for their wonderful palates, flawless attention to detail, and tireless good humor—both in and out of the kitchen.

Thanks also to Judy Bart Kancigor and Beth Hensperger for letting me bounce ideas off their very knowledgeable heads.

And especially to Susan Wyler, who always knows how to cook up a good thing.

INTRODUCTION

For your guests, a fondue party promises more than the traditional sit-down dinner. It's a communal experience that delivers action, high spirits, and fun as well as good eating. With fondue on the menu, everyone knows the evening will be relaxed. You and your guests will have time to savor each morsel and indulge in the lively conversation and amusement that helping oneself engenders. Best of all, a fondue party is the ultimate do-ahead dinner. As host, you'll get to spend plenty of time with your friends; instead of being tied to the stove, you'll be hovering right over the fondue pot with them.

With fondue, guests not only get to prepare their own food; in some measure they also get to choose what to eat, selecting which tidbits to dip and swirl and which sauces to enjoy as embellishment. Given the wide range of dietary programs around today, this makes it easier to please everyone. And it provides a tremendous variety of possible taste combinations in just one dish.

The word *fondue* derives from the French verb *fondre*, which means "to melt," and the first fondues were probably made of melted cheese. Some believe fondue originated around five hundred years ago, during the Protestant Reformation. In Switzerland, battling religious factions combined whatever provisions they had to stave off hunger: last summer's cheese (Swiss Gruyère, of course), homemade wine, and crusts of stale bread. Needless to say, fondue has come a long way since then.

The two most traditional hot dipping dishes are cheese fondue, in which the fondue itself is the focal point, and beef fondue, in which the item dipped is of prime interest. These days, the culinary world is more sophisticated and open to experimentation, so fondues, along with all other edibles, are limited only by the cook's imagination. All you need is molten cheese, a sauce, or another medium thick enough to cling to chunks of bread, vegetables, meats, or seafood—or in the case of dessert fondues, to fruits, cookies, and bits of cake.

Some of these fondues are best eaten in small bites, as a hot appetizer or as a dessert. Others, with or without accompaniment, serve as a meal in a pot. A number can go either way. Each recipe in this book indicates not only the number of servings, but how best to serve it.

While most people are familiar with traditional Swiss cheese fondue, *Great Party Fondues* explores a variety of high-quality artisanal cheeses like Spanish Manchego, French Brie, and goat and blue cheeses from California. In addition to the classic beef cooked in hot oil, this fondue collection puts tabletop sizzle into fresh seafood, chicken brochettes, tortelloni, and lamb spiedini. Some recipes—like Mushroom Stroganoff Fondue, Cauliflower Fondue with Asiago and Smoked Paprika, and Emerald Spinach Fondue—put the emphasis on fresh vegetables.

Half the fun of fondue is in the ritual; the other half, of course, is in the eating. Over the years the Swiss have developed a number of customs centered around the fondue pot. They say that if a piece of bread falls off a woman's fork into the fondue, she must kiss the man on her left. If a man drops his bread, some say he has to buy a round of drinks for the table; others insist he chugalug a full glass of wine or down a straight shot of liquor. (If this chauvinism bothers you, keep in mind this is the country that only gave all women the vote in 1971.) Depending on the house rules you establish, fondue can end up a warm, communal meal or a playful, fun-filled party. Maybe a bit of both is a good idea.

In general, the simpler the ingredients you are dipping, the more important the sauces become. It's thoughtful to offer a selection of sauces that appeal to a wide range of tastes. To make that all the more exciting, *Great Party Fondues* includes an entire chapter of zesty international sauces and condiments, like Scandinavian Mustard Sauce, Puttanesca Sauce, Sesame Peanut Sauce, and Chipotle Mayonnaise.

For dessert, the stars are fondues made of chocolate, whether it be white, dark, or milk. Recipes for sweet fondues also venture into less-explored territory with ideas like Dulce de Leche Fondue, Peanut Butter Fondue with Chocolate Swirls, Caramel Fondue with Fleur de Sel, and even a Sweet Cheese Fondue, made with mascarpone and dessert wine.

FONDUE POTS
and other equipment

There are several types of fondue pots, and different sorts of recipes really do best when served in the pot designed for them. If you enjoy fondue on a fairly regular basis or frequently serve fondue as an appetizer to large groups, it may be worth collecting an assortment of styles.

Tall, narrow pots, usually made of a light-gauge stainless steel, are fairly compact and often smaller at the top than the bottom. They are designed especially for fondues in which meat or other food is seared in hot oil. The relatively thin metal allows the flame beneath to bring the oil to a high temperature, and the shape is efficient for both warming and maintaining heat. These pots usually have a capacity no larger than 1½ quarts. A number of the newer metal pots come with a ceramic insert so they can be used for cheese and chocolate fondues as well. The only problem with this shape is that you can't get a lot of forks into the narrow opening at one time, which makes it impractical for large groups. If you're planning a party of more than four to six, you'll probably need two on the table. Also remember that the temperature of the oil drops slightly with each new piece of cold meat that is added to the pot, so you'll want to avoid overcrowding.

Some other new models feature a hard-anodized nonstick saucepan with conveniences such as a heatproof comfort-grip handle and a removable ring with indentations for holding the forks during cooking. This insert also reduces the chances of spattering. The saucepan fits into a tall stainless-steel stand with an adjustable fuel holder designed for gel or paste fuel. Although the pot is easy to carry from the stove and rests securely in the stand, guests must take care to avoid knocking the handle and thereby spilling at the table.

Heavy ceramic fondue pots, with a capacity of anywhere from 2 cups to 3 quarts, are based upon the original Swiss *caquelon,* an earthenware casserole glazed on the inside. These pots are bowl-shaped, shallower than the metal fondue pots, and may or may not have a handle. While designed especially for cheese, these work equally well for dessert fondues, as both require low, even heat. The wide opening of the casserole makes it ideal for larger parties.

Several manufacturers now offer heavy enameled cast-iron fondue pots, which rest on a sturdy cast-iron base and are designed to go from stove to tabletop. With a capacity of about 1 3/4 quarts and small handles on either side to facilitate carrying, these pots can be used for cheese, savory, and dessert fondues serving four to six people. Several brands are equipped with a removable spatter-proof insert that fits around the rim of the pot. Another nice thing about enameled cast iron is the variety of colors available. The accompanying burners are designed so you can adjust the heat—a very helpful feature—and are fueled by denatured alcohol, which is readily available at hardware stores and in many supermarkets.

Note: Almost all the recipes in this book were designed to be prepared in a saucepan and then transferred to a fondue pot. If you have one of the all-purpose, stovetop models described above, you can prepare the entire dish in one pot. Just make sure the fondue does not fill the pot more than halfway.

Die-hard fondue fans may opt for one of the newer electric pots, which allow you to control the temperature precisely. Remember, though, the cord needs to reach an electrical outlet, so safe positioning is a key factor.

Traditional chafing dishes, which have a capacity of anywhere from 1 to 3 1/2 quarts or more, can work in a pinch for cheese or dessert fondues. The shape is shallow and wider than a traditional fondue pot, making it a good choice for large groups. Chafing dishes are either heated with a candle or by a water bath kept warm with a gel fuel, such as Sterno. The latter, sometimes called canned heat, is a better choice because you can control the temperature, by removing the lid for the highest fuel output, or covering partially for gentler heat.

Small electric slow cookers, which range from 1 1/2 to 3 quarts in capacity, can be used on the low heat setting for cheese and dessert fondues. Again, there is a cord to contend with, and a certain lack of romance compared to a traditional fondue pot.

No matter what type of pot you are using, long-handled fondue forks are a must for cooking and dunking. They are traditionally two-pronged, with elongated tines to efficiently spear chunks of food. The idea is to keep the morsel on the fork, not drop it into the fondue.

Fondue forks are usually color-coded with a dot at the end of the handle so guests can keep track of their own and use the same one throughout the evening. Although fondue pots often come with four to six dishwasher-safe fondue forks, many well-stocked housewares stores sell these forks separately. If you entertain large numbers, it's a good idea to keep some extras on hand.

Bamboo skewers are another option for spearing dippers. While not as efficient as the forks at holding onto the food, they are inexpensive and can provide strength in numbers. Skewers are most appropriate for appetizer and dessert fondues, where the medium in the pot is more of a dip. If using bamboo skewers with an oil-based fondue, first soak them in water for 30 minutes to avoid scorching, then dry well to avoid splatters.

notes on INGREDIENTS

Because fondues are so simply made and the raw components are often on display, buy the best quality ingredients you can afford. The difference will be noticeable.

BREAD: Don't even bother trying to dunk presliced white bread—it will fall apart before it ever reaches your mouth. Purchase a good, chewy French or Italian loaf that will withstand the heat of the fondue and the density of the cheese. Cut it into bite-size cubes with a serrated knife, leaving the crust intact. If the bread feels too soft, lightly toast it in the oven for 5 to 10 minutes, or let it air-dry for a few hours before serving. The texture should be firm and dry but not stale.

CHEESE: Buy the best cheese you can find, preferably from a specialized cheese shop or a discriminating supermarket. Ask questions, if need be, to determine a cheese's melting potential, and taste a sample to be sure you like it a lot. As a general rule, avoid pregrated cheeses for fondue. Shred your own by hand or in a food processor, preferably the same day you will be using it.

CHOCOLATE: Unless otherwise indicated in the recipe, purchase large chunks of good-quality chocolate with high cacao content. Cut into small pieces with a sturdy serrated knife. Although it may seem easier to substitute semisweet chocolate chips, they will not provide the silky texture or intense flavor of premium chocolate needed in most of these recipes. Because chocolate fondue is so popular, for convenience some upscale retailers now carry premium chocolate wafers or special "chips" specifically made for melting.

CORNSTARCH: While purists might object, a small amount of cornstarch is often added to cheese fondue to prevent the cheese from separating when heated. It keeps the fondue smooth and amalgamated, and no one will know it's there.

FISH AND SHELLFISH: With seafood, freshness is everything. Avoid prepackaged plastic-wrapped fish, and be sure any seafood you buy smells fresh and briny. All skin and bones should be removed when fish is cut into bite-size pieces. Diners should be able to pop a piece into their mouths without concern.

KIRSCH: For cheese fondue, a bottle of good imported kirsch is a long-term investment, as it is used very sparingly. *Kirschwasser,* as it is sometimes called, is an eau-de-vie made from mountain cherries, and it is a traditional addition to classic cheese fondue. You can use another eau-de-vie you may have on hand, such as pear or raspberry, or substitute cognac or brandy.

MEAT: Bright red, fresh smelling, glossy meat is a must for fondue because it will be presented raw. Only the most tender cuts will work, and of course, it should be boneless. Be sure to trim off all excess fat and membranes. When purchasing, keep in mind that meats that are lightly marbled with fat are less likely to dry out during cooking.

OIL: Peanut oil will withstand the highest heat without smoking, but a flavorless vegetable oil may be substituted when necessary. In general, olive oil has too strong a flavor for fondue.

VEGETABLES: Most vegetables can be dunked into fondue raw, but you may want to blanch asparagus, broccoli, carrots, and cauliflower for just a minute or two in order to enhance their flavor and set the color. To do this, cut the vegetables into bite-size pieces. Bring a large pot of salted water to a boil. Add the vegetables; as soon as the water returns to a boil, lift out the vegetables with a slotted spoon and plunge immediately into a bowl of ice water to stop the cooking. Drain well before serving.

WINE: The white wine used in cheese fondue should be crisp and acidic, like the wines of Switzerland. French Loire wines, such as Sancerre and muscadet, are often acceptable, but many California chardonnays are simply too rich or "oaky," and they can overwhelm the delicate nuttiness of the cheese. If using a California wine, opt for something like a dry sauvignon blanc. In a pinch, add a small splash of lemon juice to the fondue to boost the acidity.

There are bound to be variables in cheeses and other ingredients, so be prepared to improvise. If a cheese fondue is too thin, add a bit more cheese, or a teaspoon or two of cornstarch diluted in an equal amount of water. If a cheese or dessert fondue is too thick, add more liquid, heated. If the fondue has separated, return it to the stovetop and heat, whisking until it smooths out.

FONDUE *etiquette*

The most important rule of fondue dining should be obvious, but often it is not observed: Never eat food right off the fondue fork—ever. In the case of a traditional fondue bourguignonne or other hot oil dip, the tines of the long-handled fork become burning-hot very quickly. Like a brochette skewer, the fondue fork should be regarded as a cooking implement, not a dining tool. Use the tines of a regular dining fork to slide food off the hot, long-handled fondue fork onto a plate; then eat with the dining fork, cutting the piece in half with a knife, if necessary. Besides avoiding a scalded tongue or lips, this method is also sanitary. For a large party, you may want to use disposable bamboo skewers.

In the case of cheese fondue, the accepted motion for capturing the fondue is to swirl your fork in a figure eight, stirring the fondue as you dip. No matter which kind of fondue you are dipping into, end the process with a short, slow twirl, so any excess fondue will drip back into the pot—and not onto the tablecloth.

Even if there are enough fondue forks for everyone, you may have to wait now and then for food to cook or for room in the pot to clear for dunking. Taking turns sometimes requires patience. But mind your manners and don't monopolize the fondue pot. When other guests are waiting for an opportunity to dunk and swirl, don't make them wait for you to fill your plate. Everyone will be anxiously awaiting their turn.

Fondues tend to go two ways. Either there are several ingredients to dunk into one medium, or there is one ingredient that is cooked and then dipped into a choice of sauces and condiments. Depending on how it is arranged, raw food is usually best taken one piece at a time from a platter. With bread cubes, vegetables, and cooked food, guests can help themselves to a few pieces or an assortment of tidbits and then dip them from their plates into the pot when ready.

Positioning an assortment of sauces so there's not a lot of reaching and passing can pose a challenge. If your guests adhere to the rule of not eating off their fondue fork, they can dip into a communal bowl before transferring the food to their plate. It's a lot more fun to have your own sauces, though, so you can mix and match as you please. This can be accomplished two ways: Small ladles or spoons in every bowl will encourage guests to dish out a little bit of each sauce onto their plate. Or—better if you can swing it—purchase a collection of small soy sauce dishes or tiny glass prep bowls and put a few at each place. You can portion out the sauces beforehand, or guests can help themselves from larger bowls on the table.

FONDUE *safety tips*

► Fill any fondue pot no more than halfway. An overfilled fondue pot is an invitation to disaster; it is far safer to return the pot to the kitchen periodically to refill.

► It's more hygienic—and appetizing—to keep meats and seafood arranged on their own chilled platters, separate from vegetables, bread cubes, and other less perishable foods. Increase visual appeal by garnishing those platters with sprigs of fresh herbs, sturdy greens like kale and mustard greens, or fresh lemon, lime, or orange.

► Cutting food into bite-size pieces carries two benefits: it eliminates the need for knives and removes any temptation for guests to double-dip.

► Young children, who are usually enthusiastic dunkers, should be closely monitored, because you're literally playing with fire here. To avoid mishaps, ladle some of the warm cheese or dessert fondue into small ramekins for individual "pint-size" dipping—far away from an open flame. Only older children—with adult supervision—should ever be allowed to cook meat in a fondue pot filled with hot oil.

► With the exception of oil-based fondues, it is best to heat fondue in a saucepan on top of the stove until it reaches the proper temperature and consistency, and then transfer it to a warm fondue pot for serving. The simplest way to preheat a fondue pot is to fill it with hot tap water. When the fondue is ready, pour out the water and wipe the pot dry before filling.

► Position the fondue pot on the table so guests will have safe, easy access to it. Be sure the pot is resting securely on its stand. A trivet or hot pad to protect your table is always a good idea.

► Don't add fuel to the fire. Before you begin serving, fill the fuel container to maximum capacity, according to the manufacturer's directions. Once it is lit, you cannot safely add more fuel.

► Fondue can get messy, especially when guests are not paying close attention to what they are doing, so don't use your favorite heirloom tablecloth. Supply plenty of napkins to mop up drips and discreetly remove dropped ingredients from the table.

CHEESE *fondues*

classic SWISS FONDUE

It's always risky to call a recipe "classic," since the most popular, time-tested dishes can be made in a variety of ways. But the three cheeses used here are indeed the great cheeses of Switzerland, and they make a fine fondue. Cubes of crusty French or Italian bread are the traditional accompaniment for dipping, but assorted vegetables and crisp apple slices make a nice addition.

► *Makes about 5 cups; 6 to 8 main-course or 12 to 14 appetizer servings*

---

1 pound Gruyère cheese, shredded

¾ pound Emmenthaler (Swiss) cheese, shredded

¼ pound Appenzeller cheese, shredded or cut into small pieces

1½ tablespoons cornstarch

1 large garlic clove, crushed with the flat side of a knife

1½ cups dry white wine

2 teaspoons fresh lemon juice

2 tablespoons kirsch (cherry eau-de-vie)

Dash of freshly grated nutmeg

Dash of cayenne pepper

1 In a large bowl, toss the shredded Gruyère, Emmenthaler, and Appenzeller cheeses with the cornstarch to coat.

2 Rub the inside of a large saucepan with the garlic and discard. Pour the wine and lemon juice into the pan and cook over medium heat until hot but not boiling. Reduce the heat to low and gradually stir in the cheese mixture, letting each addition melt before adding more. Stir in the kirsch and cook for 2 minutes longer. Season with the nutmeg and cayenne.

3 Transfer to a fondue pot, preferably ceramic or enameled cast iron, and serve at once. Regulate the heat under the pot, if possible, so that the cheese fondue remains warm, not hot.

BRIE FONDUE *with crab and champagne*

A New Year's celebration would be the perfect time to present this lavish fondue, which is as easy as it is elegant. The most time-consuming part is trimming the rind from the cheese. (Although edible, the rind will not melt completely, and it lends an unpleasant flavor to fondue.) If you have any flat, leftover champagne, use it here. Look for a young, fresh Brie with few striations in the rind and no smell of ammonia. Serve with bread cubes or sticks, tiny roasted artichoke hearts, Belgian endive leaves, steamed fingerling potatoes, or asparagus spears.

► *Makes about 3½ cups; 8 to 10 appetizer servings*

- 1½ tablespoons unsalted butter
- 2 tablespoons finely chopped shallots
- 1 tablespoon all-purpose flour
- 1¼ cups brut champagne or sparkling wine
- 1 tablespoon fresh lemon juice
- 1 pound Brie cheese, well chilled, rind removed, cheese cut into small cubes
- 8 ounces crabmeat, drained well and picked over to remove any shell or bits of cartilage
- Dash of cayenne pepper
- Salt
- 1 tablespoon minced fresh chives

1 In a medium saucepan, melt the butter over medium heat. Add the shallots and cook, stirring occasionally, until softened but not browned, 1 to 2 minutes. Stir in the flour and cook, stirring frequently, for 1 to 2 minutes, without allowing it to color. Whisk in the champagne and lemon juice. Bring to a boil, whisking until thickened and smooth. Reduce the heat to low and simmer for 2 to 3 minutes.

2 Gradually stir in the Brie, letting each addition melt before adding more. Stir in the crab and cayenne. Season with a dash of salt if needed.

3 Transfer to a fondue pot, preferably ceramic or enameled cast iron, and sprinkle the chives over the top. Regulate the heat under the pot, if possible, so that the cheese fondue remains warm, not hot.

CREAMY MANCHEGO FONDUE *with smoked paprika*

Pimentón de la Vera is a paprika made from sweet red peppers naturally smoked over oak fires. If you can't find the authentic item, commercial spice lines now carry a generic smoked paprika. Dip cubes of ciabatta or walnut bread into this fondue along with chunks of smoked chorizo, thinly sliced serrano ham, jarred pickled vegetables, fresh or dried figs, and tiny roasted new potatoes. In keeping with the Spanish theme, set out bowls of Marcona almonds and olives for nibbling.

► *Makes about 3 cups; 4 main-course or 8 to 10 appetizer servings*

---

1 pound manchego cheese, shredded

1 tablespoon cornstarch

1 large garlic clove, crushed with the flat side of a knife

1¼ cups light cream or half-and-half

1 tablespoon fresh lemon juice

1 tablespoon brandy or dry sherry

½ to 1 teaspoon sweet or bittersweet *pimentón de la Vera* or other smoked paprika

Salt and freshly ground black pepper

1 In a large bowl, toss the cheese with the cornstarch to coat.

2 Rub the inside of a large saucepan with the garlic and discard. Add the light cream to the pan and warm over medium heat, watching carefully, until hot but not boiling. Reduce the heat to low and gradually stir in the cheese mixture, letting each addition melt before adding more. Season with the lemon juice, brandy, smoked paprika, and salt and pepper to taste.

3 Transfer to a fondue pot, preferably ceramic or enameled cast iron, and serve at once. Regulate the heat under the pot, if possible, so that the cheese fondue remains warm, not hot.

BLUE FONDUE *with a kiss of cognac*

Well, the fondue here isn't really blue, but the cheese is. Look for a good artisanal blue, such as one of our wonderful American artisanal blue cheeses, like that made in California by the Point Reyes Farmstead Cheese Company. An all-blue fondue would be too intense; cream cheese and light cream take off the edge. For the cream cheese, it's better to use the bulk type sold in the deli section than the packaged kind. Buffalo wings would be a natural accompaniment here. Other dippers might include Asian pear slices, dried figs, celery sticks, cherry tomatoes, oven-roasted mushrooms, crisp hearts of romaine lettuce, cubes of cooked ham, and, of course, crusty bread cubes.

► *Makes about 3½ cups; 8 to 10 appetizer servings*

---

1 large garlic clove, crushed with the flat side of a knife

1 cup light cream or half-and-half

2 tablespoons cognac or brandy

1 tablespoon cornstarch

1 pound blue cheese, crumbled

8 ounces cream cheese, preferably the bulk variety, cut into bits

1½ teaspoons chopped fresh thyme or ½ teaspoon dried thyme leaves

Cayenne pepper

1 Rub the inside of a medium saucepan with the garlic and discard. Add the light cream to the pan and warm over medium heat.

2 In a small bowl, whisk together the cognac and cornstarch until well blended. Whisk into the warm cream. Bring to a boil, stirring, until smooth and slightly thickened, about 3 minutes. Reduce the heat to low and gradually stir in the blue cheese and cream cheese, letting each addition melt before adding more. Stir in the thyme and cayenne to taste.

3 Transfer to a fondue pot, preferably ceramic or enameled cast iron, and serve at once. Regulate the heat under the pot, if possible, so that the cheese fondue remains warm, not hot.

GOUDA AND CHEDDAR *fondue*

Children love to dip, and things only get better when gooey cheese is involved. Instead of wine, this fondue gets its sparkle from apple cider, making it totally kid friendly. For small children unable to maneuver long forks or resist the lure of an open flame, it's best to ladle small portions of fondue into individual ramekins. As they dip their bowls clean, an adult can ladle warm refills from the fondue pot. Serve this with pita triangles, bread sticks, pretzels, baby carrots, broccoli florets (also known, for picky eaters, as "little trees"), apple slices (tossed in a little lemon juice to prevent darkening), and dried apricots.

► *Makes about 4 cups; 4 to 6 main-course or 10 to 12 appetizer servings*

---

1 pound young Gouda cheese, shredded

8 ounces natural cheddar cheese, shredded

1½ tablespoons cornstarch

1½ teaspoons powdered mustard, such as Colman's

1½ cups unsweetened apple cider or apple juice

1½ tablespoons fresh lemon juice

Dash of freshly grated nutmeg

1 In a large bowl, toss the Gouda and cheddar cheese with the cornstarch and powdered mustard to coat.

2 In a medium saucepan, heat the apple cider and lemon juice until hot but not boiling. Reduce the heat to low and gradually stir in the cheese mixture, letting each addition melt before adding more. Season with the nutmeg.

3 Transfer to a fondue pot, preferably ceramic or enameled cast iron, and serve at once. Regulate the heat under the pot, if possible, so that the cheese fondue remains warm, not hot.

JALAPEÑO JACK
fiesta fondue

What this Southwestern-style fondue may lack in sophistication, it makes up for in Wild West flavor. A generous hit of tequila blends with cayenne for a perfect kick. It's ideal with margaritas on the patio in summer, or in front of the television during fall football games. Try dipping chunks of cooked chicken breast, sausage, meatballs, or shellfish, or any combination of crisp vegetables. Instead of bread cubes, consider serving warm flour tortillas or sturdy corn chips.

► *Makes about 5½ cups; 6 to 8 main-course or 12 to 14 appetizer servings*

---

2 pounds pepper Jack cheese, shredded

2 tablespoons cornstarch

2 bottles (12 ounces each) beer, preferably Mexican

1 large garlic clove, minced

¼ teaspoon cayenne pepper

⅓ cup tequila

1 In a large bowl, toss the shredded cheese with the cornstarch to coat.

2 In a large saucepan, combine the beer, garlic, and cayenne. Cook over medium heat until the beer is heated through and begins to bubble around the edges. Reduce the heat to low and gradually stir in the cheese mixture, letting each addition melt before adding more. Stir in the tequila and cook, stirring, for 1 minute longer.

3 Transfer to a fondue pot, preferably ceramic or enameled cast iron, and serve at once. Regulate the heat under the pot, if possible, so that the cheese fondue remains warm, not hot.

CHEDDAR CHEESE *fondue*

Sometimes simplicity speaks louder than embellishment. In this recipe, natural cheddar cheese—which is cream colored rather than dyed orange—is combined with beer and only a few other ingredients for a surprising burst of silky goodness. Try to remember to open the beer about an hour ahead of time, to reduce the amount of foam; flat beer is preferable for this recipe.

► *Makes about 5 cups; 6 to 8 main-course or 12 to 14 appetizer servings*

---

2 pounds aged cheddar cheese, shredded

2 tablespoons cornstarch

1 teaspoon powdered mustard, such as Colman's

2 tablespoons unsalted butter

2 cups beer

1 teaspoon Worcestershire sauce

¼ teaspoon hot pepper sauce

1 In a large bowl, toss the cheese with the cornstarch and powdered mustard to coat.

2 In a large saucepan, melt the butter in the beer over medium-high heat. Bring to a boil, reduce the heat to low, and gradually stir in the cheese mixture, letting each addition melt before adding more. Stir in the Worcestershire and hot sauce.

3 Transfer to a fondue pot, preferably ceramic or enameled cast iron, and serve at once. Regulate the heat underneath the pot, if possible, to keep the fondue warm, not hot.

FONTINA FONDUE *with fennel and olives*

Fennel's subtle anise flavor and the pleasant bite of olives complement the nuttiness of mild fontina and Gruyère, and provide a nice textural element. Here I've used Italian Cerignola olives, which are large and meaty, but any green olive will do. If the fennel bulbs you purchase still have fresh feathery fronds attached, chop and reserve a tablespoon or so to garnish the top of the fondue. Raw fennel stalks can be used for dipping, along with cubes of plain focaccia or other Italian bread, squares of firm polenta, Belgian endive leaves, sliced salami, bites of cooked boneless chicken breast, roasted whole cremini mushrooms, and broccoli florets.

► *Makes about 4 cups; 4 to 6 main-course or 10 to 12 appetizer servings*

---

1 tablespoon unsalted butter

2 small fennel bulbs (about 1¼ pounds total), trimmed, halved, and thinly sliced

Salt and freshly ground black pepper

8 ounces Italian fontina cheese, shredded

8 ounces Gruyère cheese, shredded

4 teaspoons cornstarch

1 cup dry white wine

¼ cup Cerignola or other brine-cured green olives, pitted and chopped

1 tablespoon Italian grappa, brandy, or fresh lemon juice

1 In a large skillet, melt the butter over medium heat. Add the fennel and cook, stirring occasionally, until softened but not browned, 8 to 10 minutes. Season lightly with salt and pepper.

2 Meanwhile, in a large bowl, toss the shredded fontina and Gruyère cheeses with the cornstarch to coat.

3 In a large saucepan, warm the wine over medium heat until hot but not boiling. Reduce the heat to low and gradually stir in the shredded cheese mixture, letting each addition melt before adding more. Stir in the cooked fennel, the olives, and the grappa, and cook for 1 minute longer.

4 Transfer to a fondue pot, preferably ceramic or enameled cast iron, and serve at once. Regulate the heat under the pot, if possible, so that the cheese fondue remains warm, not hot.

MOZZARELLA SURPRISE

marinara fondue

This simmering pot of tomato sauce may look ordinary, but curious diners who swirl bits of bread deep into the pot will be rewarded with a gooey bonus of mozzarella cheese. Not the rubbery stuff found on delivery pizza, mind you, but the ethereal luxury of fresh whole-milk mozzarella. Look for it in cheese shops, Italian delis, and well-stocked supermarkets. Serve the fondue with crusty Italian bread cubes, bread sticks, firm polenta squares, skewers of cooked tortellini or ravioli, oven-roasted whole mushrooms, or fried zucchini.

► *Makes about 4 cups; 4 to 6 main-course or 10 to 12 appetizer servings*

---

3 tablespoons extra virgin olive oil

1 small onion, finely chopped

1 tablespoon tomato paste

2 garlic cloves, minced

1 can (28 ounces) crushed tomatoes with basil

½ cup full-bodied dry red wine, such as zinfandel

½ teaspoon salt

¼ teaspoon crushed hot red pepper

⅛ teaspoon sugar

1 tablespoon chopped fresh basil

1 tablespoon chopped fresh parsley

8 ounces fresh mozzarella cheese, cut into ½-inch pieces

1 In a large nonreactive skillet, warm the olive oil over medium heat. Add the onion and cook, stirring often, until softened but not browned, 3 to 5 minutes. Add the tomato paste and garlic and cook, stirring, for 1 minute.

2 Stir in the tomatoes with their juices, the wine, salt, hot pepper, and sugar. Bring to a boil, reduce the heat, and simmer, stirring occasionally, until the marinara sauce is slightly thickened, 8 to 10 minutes. Add the basil and parsley. Season with additional salt if needed.

3 Scatter the pieces of cheese evenly over the bottom of a fondue pot, preferably ceramic or enameled cast iron. Pour the marinara sauce over the top. Regulate the heat under the pot, if possible, so that the cheese fondue remains warm, not hot.

TRUFFLED JARLSBERG *and wild mushroom fondue*

Norway's Jarlsberg cheese is mild and buttery. Here I've boosted its flavor by adding a bit of Parmesan, to be sure it stands up to the woodsy flavors of wild mushrooms, and, for the final touch of umami, a drizzling of fragrant truffle oil. Serve this rich-tasting fondue with crusty bread cubes, tiny roasted new potatoes and artichoke hearts, cubes of firm polenta, Belgian endive leaves, or assorted raw vegetables.

► *Makes about 3½ cups; 4 to 6 main-course or 8 to 10 appetizer servings*

---

3 tablespoons unsalted butter

12 ounces fresh wild mushrooms, such as shiitake, porcini, morels, or chanterelles, or a combination of wild and cultivated cremini or white mushrooms, finely chopped (see Note)

2 teaspoons chopped fresh thyme or ½ teaspoon dried thyme leaves

¼ teaspoon salt

⅛ teaspoon freshly ground black pepper

1 pound Jarlsberg cheese, shredded

¼ cup freshly grated Parmesan cheese

4 teaspoons cornstarch

1 cup dry white wine

1 tablespoon fresh lemon juice

1 teaspoon black or white truffle oil

1 In a large skillet, melt the butter over medium-high heat. Add the mushrooms and cook, stirring occasionally, until they give off their liquid and begin to brown, 5 to 7 minutes. Season with the thyme, salt, and pepper.

2 Meanwhile, in a large bowl, toss the shredded Jarlsberg and grated Parmesan cheese with the cornstarch to coat.

3 In a large saucepan, warm the wine and lemon juice over medium heat until hot but not boiling. Reduce the heat to low and gradually stir in the cheese mixture, letting each addition melt before adding more. Stir in the mushrooms and cook for 1 minute longer. Season with additional salt and pepper to taste.

4 Transfer to a fondue pot, preferably ceramic or enameled cast iron, and drizzle the truffle oil over the top. Regulate the heat under the pot, if possible, so that the cheese fondue remains warm, not hot.

Note: If wild mushrooms are unavailable or prohibitively expensive, substitute 4 ounces of chopped fresh cremini or white mushrooms along with 2 ounces of assorted dried wild mushrooms that have been rehydrated in warm water for about 20 minutes, drained well, and chopped.

GOAT CHEESE FONDUE *with sun-dried tomatoes and rosemary*

As with blue cheese, the flavor of an all-goat-cheese fondue would be a bit overwhelming, so it's best to neutralize it with cream cheese. Goat cheese is particularly sensitive to heat, so keep the flame as low as possible to prevent the texture from becoming grainy. Serve with cubes of plain focaccia or olive bread, bread sticks, crostini, crisp hearts of romaine lettuce, broccoli florets, squares of firm polenta, and bites of cooked boneless chicken breast.

► *Makes about 3 cups; 8 to 10 appetizer servings*

---

1 large garlic clove, crushed with the flat side of a knife

1 cup light cream or half-and-half

4 teaspoons cornstarch

1 tablespoon fresh lemon juice

8 ounces cream cheese, cut into bits

8 ounces soft white goat cheese, crumbled

⅓ cup oil-packed sun-dried tomato halves, drained, blotted dry, and finely chopped

1 tablespoon finely chopped fresh rosemary or 1 teaspoon dried

Salt and freshly ground black pepper

1 Rub the inside of a medium saucepan with the garlic and discard. Add the light cream to the pan and warm over medium heat.

2 In a small bowl, whisk together the cornstarch and lemon juice with 1 ½ tablespoons of water until well blended. Whisk into the warm cream. Bring to a boil, stirring, until smooth and slightly thickened, 3 to 5 minutes. Reduce the heat to low and gradually stir in the cream cheese and then the goat cheese, letting each addition melt before adding more. Stir in the sun-dried tomatoes and rosemary. Season with salt and pepper to taste.

3 Transfer to a fondue pot, preferably ceramic or enameled cast iron, and serve at once. Regulate the heat under the pot, if possible, so that the cheese fondue remains warm, not hot.

GRUYÈRE FONDUE *with caramelized onions*

Sweet caramelized onions, in tandem with a fragrant blend of dried herbs, provide a pleasing backdrop for nutty Gruyère in this variation on the classic Swiss cheese fondue. If you prefer a milder fondue, substitute another Swiss cheese for part of the Gruyère. Serve with crusty cubes of rosemary bread, bite-size pieces of cooked beef, chicken, or sausage, oven-roasted whole mushrooms, fennel slices, and other crisp vegetables.

► *Makes about 4½ cups; 4 to 6 main-course or 10 to 12 appetizer servings*

---

2 tablespoons unsalted butter

1 tablespoon olive oil

2 large onions, halved and thinly sliced

¾ teaspoon herbes de Provence

Salt and freshly ground black pepper

1½ pounds Gruyère cheese, shredded

1½ tablespoons cornstarch

1 large garlic clove, crushed with the flat side of a knife

1½ cups dry white wine

1 tablespoon white wine vinegar

Dash of cayenne pepper

1 In a large skillet, melt the butter in the oil over medium-low heat. Stir in the onions, herbes de Provence, ¼ teaspoon salt, and pepper to taste. Cover the skillet and cook for 5 minutes. Uncover and continue to cook, stirring occasionally, until the onions are soft and golden brown, 35 to 45 minutes longer.

2 In a large bowl, toss the shredded Gruyère cheese with the cornstarch to coat.

3 Rub the inside of a medium saucepan with the garlic and discard. Add the wine, vinegar, and cayenne to the pan. Cook over medium heat until hot but not boiling. Reduce the heat to low and gradually stir in the cheese mixture, letting each addition melt before adding more. Add all but about ½ cup of the onions. Season with additional salt and pepper to taste.

4 Transfer to a fondue pot, preferably ceramic or enameled cast iron, and scatter the remaining onions on top. Regulate the heat under the pot, if possible, so that the cheese fondue remains warm, not hot.

PARMESAN FONDUE
with pesto

For the creamiest results, purchase natural cream cheese without any added gum arabic or other stabilizers. It's sold in bulk in the deli section of the supermarket. And for best flavor, use a top-quality imported Parmesan cheese, Parmigiano-Reggiano. Both are widely available at cheese shops, delicatessens, and many upscale supermarkets. Serve this rich fondue with cubes of crusty artisanal bread and crisp raw vegetables.

► *Makes about 4 cups; 10 to 12 appetizer servings*

---

1 pound cream cheese, preferably the bulk variety

2 cups light cream or half-and-half

1½ cups freshly grated Parmesan cheese (about 6 ounces)

Dash of salt

Dash of cayenne pepper

⅓ cup basil pesto, purchased or homemade

1 Melt the cream cheese in the top of a double boiler or a large heatproof bowl set over a pan of simmering water. Gradually stir in the light cream until smooth and heated through. Add the Parmesan and stir until the cheese melts and thickens the fondue. Season with the salt and cayenne.

2 Transfer the mixture to a fondue pot, preferably ceramic or enameled cast iron. Drop teaspoons of pesto over the top; then use a skewer or a knife to swirl the pesto attractively over the surface. Regulate the heat under the pot, if possible, so that the cheese fondue remains warm, not hot.

SAUSAGE PIZZA *fondue*

Imagine if the topping of your favorite pizza remained warm and gooey no matter how many slices you ate. That should give you an idea what this friendly fondue is all about. Crusty Italian bread cubes, strips of plain focaccia, and sesame breadsticks make fine dippers, along with crisp raw vegetables. Because of the assertive flavors in this fondue, it's okay to take a shortcut by using a packaged shredded cheese blend.

► *Makes about 4½ cups; 4 to 6 main-course or 10 to 12 appetizer servings*

---

1 pound shredded Italian cheese blend, such as mozzarella, provolone, and Parmesan (about 4 cups total)

1 tablespoon cornstarch

1 tablespoon extra-virgin olive oil

½ pound sweet Italian sausage (see Note), casings removed

2 cups prepared pizza sauce

1 tablespoon balsamic vinegar

1 large garlic clove, minced

⅛ teaspoon crushed hot red pepper

½ cup pitted Kalamata olives, coarsely chopped

2 teaspoons chopped fresh oregano, or ½ teaspoon dried

1 In a large bowl, toss the shredded cheese with the cornstarch to coat.

2 In a large skillet, heat the olive oil over medium-high heat. Crumble the sausage into the skillet and cook, stirring occasionally, until lightly browned with no trace of pink, 5 to 7 minutes. Remove with a slotted spoon and drain on paper towels. Discard any fat remaining in the skillet, but do not wash.

3 In the same skillet, combine the pizza sauce, balsamic vinegar, garlic, and hot pepper flakes. Cook over medium heat, scraping up any browned bits from the bottom of the pan, until the sauce is heated through, 3 to 5 minutes. Reduce the heat to low and gradually stir in the cheese mixture, letting each addition melt before adding more.

4 Stir in the olives and oregano. Transfer to a fondue pot, preferably ceramic or enameled cast iron, and serve at once. Regulate the heat under the pot, if possible, so that the cheese fondue remains warm, not hot.

Note: If you like your food spicy, use half sweet and half hot Italian sausage

SOUTHWESTERN *chile cheese* FONDUE

This fondue blends Monterey Jack and cheddar cheese with light cream, cream cheese, and plenty of Southwestern flavor. Offer sturdy tortilla chips, warm flour tortillas, chunks of cooked chorizo sausage, and plenty of crunchy fresh vegetables as dippers.

► *Makes about 5 cups; 6 to 8 main-course or 12 to 14 appetizer servings*

---

8 ounces Monterey Jack cheese, shredded

8 ounces sharp cheddar cheese, shredded

1 tablespoon cornstarch

1½ tablespoons vegetable oil

1 medium onion, finely chopped

1 red bell pepper, finely diced

2 tomatoes, seeded and finely chopped, or 1 can (14½ ounces) petite cut diced tomatoes, well drained

2 or 3 jalapeño or serrano chile peppers, seeded and minced

1 large garlic clove, minced

2 cups light cream or half-and-half

6 ounces cream cheese, at room temperature

1 tablespoon fresh lime juice

1 In a large bowl, toss the Monterey Jack and cheddar cheese with the cornstarch to coat.

2 In a large skillet, heat the oil over medium heat. Add the onion and bell pepper and cook, stirring occasionally, until the onion is softened but not browned, about 5 minutes. Stir in the tomatoes, chile peppers, and garlic and cook, stirring occasionally, until most of the moisture evaporates, about 5 minutes. Pour in the light cream and cook, stirring, until the sauce just reaches a boil. Reduce the heat to low.

3 Break the cream cheese into small pieces and gradually stir into the hot chile-tomato sauce until melted and smooth. Gradually stir in the shredded cheese mixture, letting each addition melt before adding more. Stir in the lime juice, cumin, and cayenne. Taste, adding salt if needed.

(continued)

1 teaspoon ground cumin

⅛ teaspoon cayenne pepper, or to taste

Salt

2 tablespoons chopped fresh cilantro and/or scallions

4 Transfer to a fondue pot, preferably ceramic or enameled cast iron. Sprinkle the cilantro and scallions over the top and serve at once. Regulate the heat under the pot, if possible, so that the cheese fondue remains warm, not hot.

WELSH *rarebit*

It seems every food historian has a theory on how this melted cheese dish got its peculiar name. The fact that it comes from a nation known for dishes like Toad in the Hole and Bubble and Squeak should be explanation enough. Serve with toasted bread or English muffins, bread sticks, cubes of cooked ham or sausage, or sturdy vegetables like cauliflower and broccoli florets.

► *Makes about 4 cups; 4 to 6 main-course or 10 to 12 appetizer servings*

- 4 slices of bacon
- 1 pound sharp aged cheddar cheese, shredded
- 1½ tablespoons cornstarch
- 1 teaspoon powdered mustard, such as Colman's
- 1 tablespoon unsalted butter
- 1 cup flat beer or ale
- 1 can (14½ ounces) petite cut diced tomatoes, well drained
- 1 teaspoon Worcestershire sauce
- ⅛ teaspoon cayenne pepper

1. Place the bacon between two double sheets of microwave-safe paper towels and microwave on high for 3 to 4 minutes, turning the slices over once, until the bacon is lightly browned and fairly crisp. Chop the bacon into bits.

2. In a large bowl, toss the cheddar cheese with the cornstarch and powdered mustard to coat.

3. In a medium saucepan, melt the butter in the beer over medium heat. Bring to a boil, reduce the heat to low, and gradually stir in the cheese mixture, letting each addition melt before adding more. Stir in the diced tomatoes, bacon, Worcestershire, and cayenne. Cook for 1 minute longer, or until heated through.

4. Transfer to a fondue pot, preferably ceramic or enameled cast iron, and serve at once. Regulate the heat under the pot, if possible, so that the cheese fondue remains warm, not hot.

RACLETTE *fondue*

Raclette is a Swiss cow's milk cheese similar to Gruyère. A dish of the same name is made by warming a hunk of the cheese over an open fire or on a cast-iron grill. As the outside melts, each diner scrapes off individual portions to eat with steamed new potatoes, tiny boiled onions, pieces of dark bread, thinly sliced cured meats, such as *bresaola* or prosciutto, and cornichons or other pickled vegetables. An easier way to enjoy a similar feast (without traveling to a ski lodge in the Alps) is to make fondue from the very same cheese and offer the same accompaniments.

Makes about 4 cups; 4 to 6 main-course or 10 to 12 appetizer servings

---

1½ pounds raclette cheese, shredded

1½ tablespoons cornstarch

1 large garlic clove, crushed with the flat side of a knife

1½ cups dry white wine

1½ tablespoons fresh lemon juice

⅛ teaspoon cayenne pepper

3 tablespoons kirsch or brandy

1 In a large bowl, toss the shredded raclette cheese with the cornstarch to coat.

2 Rub the inside of a medium saucepan with the garlic and discard. Add the wine, lemon juice, and cayenne to the pan. Cook over medium heat until hot but not boiling. Reduce the heat to low and gradually stir in the cheese mixture, letting each addition melt before adding more. Stir in the kirsch and cook for 2 minutes longer.

3 Transfer to a fondue pot, preferably ceramic or enameled cast iron, and serve at once. Regulate the heat under the pot, if possible, so that the cheese fondue remains warm, not hot.

SAVORY *fondues*

chipotle SWEET POTATO FONDUE

Forget the brown sugar and gooey marshmallows—this is the way to give sweet potatoes the respect they deserve. My friend Carol Henry Prata is an inspired cook who generally leans toward healthy choices, but never at the expense of flavor. This zesty combination may just be one of her finest moments in the kitchen. Serve with chilled cooked shrimp, chunks of crusty Italian bread, and assorted crudités for dipping.

► *Makes about 4 cups; 10 to 12 appetizer servings*

---

1 tablespoon unsalted butter

1 medium onion, chopped

1½ pounds sweet potatoes, peeled and cut into 1½-inch chunks

2½ cups chicken broth

1 teaspoon finely chopped canned chipotle chile in adobo sauce

½ cup plus 1½ tablespoons crème fraîche or sour cream

1 tablespoon freshly squeezed lime juice

Salt

1 tablespoon coarsely chopped fresh cilantro or parsley

1 In a large saucepan, melt the butter over medium heat. Add the onion and cook, stirring occasionally, until softened but not browned, 3 to 5 minutes.

2 Add the sweet potatoes and enough of the chicken broth to cover. Increase the heat to medium-high and bring to a boil. Reduce the heat to medium-low and cook, partially covered, until the sweet potatoes are tender when pierced with the tip of a sharp knife, about 20 minutes.

3 Remove the pan from the heat. Using a handheld immersion blender, puree the sweet potatoes in the broth until smooth. Alternatively, puree in batches in a blender or food processor until smooth, and return the sweet potatoes to the saucepan. Beat in the chipotle chile.

4 Whisk in ½ cup of the crème fraîche and the lime juice. If the mixture is too thick, whisk in a little additional broth or water. Season with salt to taste.

(continued)

Cook over medium-low heat until heated through, about 5 minutes.

5 Transfer to a ceramic or enameled cast iron fondue pot. Drizzle the remaining 1½ tablespoons crème fraîche on top and sprinkle with the cilantro. Regulate the heat under the pot, if possible, so that the fondue remains warm, not hot.

creamy BAGNA CAUDA

Northern Italians soften their *bagna cauda* with butter and cream or milk. Not a bad idea, since this recipe contains an entire head of garlic. Serve it with a basket of raw vegetables and another basket of bread. Swirl the vegetables in the sauce, then hold a slice of bread under the vegetables as an edible napkin to catch any delicious drips.

► *Makes about 3 cups; 10 to 12 appetizer servings*

---

2 sticks (8 ounces) unsalted butter, cut into pieces

1 medium head of garlic, peeled and coarsely chopped

2 tins (2 ounces each) flat anchovy fillets, drained and chopped

2 cups light cream or half-and-half

Dash of salt

1 In a medium saucepan, melt 1 stick of the butter over medium-low heat. Add the garlic and cook, stirring, until softened and fragrant but not browned, about 3 minutes.

2 Add the anchovies and reduce the heat to low. Cook, stirring, until the anchovies dissolve into a paste, 1 to 2 minutes. Add the remaining butter, the cream, and the salt. Cook, stirring occasionally, until the butter melts and the *bagna cauda* is heated through, about 5 minutes.

3 Transfer to a ceramic or enameled cast-iron fondue pot and serve at once. Regulate the heat under the pot, if possible, so the fondue remains warm, not hot.

CAULIFLOWER FONDUE *with asiago and smoked paprika*

If you don't announce the name of this fondue, most people will be hard-pressed to identify the main ingredient. Serve this creamy vegetable dip with cubes of crusty whole-grain bread and an assortment of oven-roasted vegetables, like tiny red-skinned new potatoes, baby carrots, large squares of red bell pepper, and zucchini chunks.

► *Makes about 3 cups; 10 to 12 appetizer servings*

---

1 head of cauliflower (about 1½ pounds), cut into 1-inch florets

1 cup heavy cream

2 tablespoons unsalted butter, cut into pieces, at room temperature

2 teaspoons fresh lemon juice

¾ teaspoon salt

½ teaspoon smoked paprika

½ cup freshly grated Asiago cheese

1 In a large saucepan fitted with a steamer basket, bring about 2 inches of water to a boil over high heat. Add the cauliflower florets, cover, and cook until the florets are very tender when pierced with the tip of a sharp knife, 8 to 10 minutes. Let cool for 5 minutes.

2 In a food processor or blender, combine half of the cauliflower and half of the cream. Pulse until the cauliflower is finely chopped. Repeat, adding the remaining florets and cream to the chopped cauliflower and scraping down the sides of the bowl with a rubber spatula. Add the butter, lemon juice, salt, and smoked paprika, and puree until smooth. Add the cheese and blend well.

3 Return the cauliflower puree to the saucepan and cook over medium-low heat, stirring occasionally, until heated through, about 5 minutes.

4 Transfer to a fondue pot, preferably enameled cast iron, and serve at once. Regulate the heat under the pot, if possible, so that the fondue remains warm, not hot.

crudité FONDUE

For a lively party, rather than offer your guests the usual chilled crudités and dip, consider this tempting and colorful fondue. A quick dunk in hot oil tenderizes vegetables, intensifies their natural flavors, and gives them an appealing golden cast—like tempura without the batter. For added zip, they get a second dip in salt seasoned with *zahtar*, a Middle Eastern spice blend of sesame seeds, powdered sumac, and dried thyme. A large, colorful array of the season's best produce is in order here. In addition to the seasoned salt, serve a few sauces for dipping, such as Madras Curry Mayonnaise (page 116), Spicy Orange-Ginger Dipping Sauce (page 117), and Cucumber-Yogurt Sauce with Dill (page 121).

Makes 10 to 12 appetizer servings

---

3 tablespoons fleur de sel or other coarse salt

2 tablespoons *zahtar*

⅛ teaspoon cayenne pepper

About 10 cups assorted fresh vegetables, such as:

Asparagus tips, trimmed to 3 to 4 inches long

Bell peppers (red, yellow, or green), cut into ¾-inch strips

Broccoli florets

Carrot sticks or baby carrots halved lengthwise

Cauliflower florets

Eggplant, cut into ¾-inch cubes

Fennel, cut into ¾-inch sticks

1 In a small bowl, combine the salt, *zahtar,* and cayenne. Stir to blend.

2 Whether they are raw or cooked, pat all the vegetables dry with paper towels. Arrange them decoratively on a large platter.

3 Pour the peanut oil into a metal fondue pot, making sure not to fill it more than halfway. Set over medium-high heat until the oil registers 375°F on a deep-frying thermometer. Carefully transfer the pot of hot oil to a fondue burner with a high flame. Have each guest spear a vegetable and cook until golden on the outside and crisp-tender, 3 to 4 minutes for the eggplant, and 1 to 3 minutes for the other vegetables. Along with your choice of sauces, offer tiny bowls of seasoned salt for dipping.

Green beans, trimmed into 2-inch lengths

Small whole mushrooms, trimmed

Small new potatoes, steamed until tender, halved or quartered

Scallions, trimmed to 3 inches long

Zucchini sticks or ¾-inch-thick slices

2 cups peanut or vegetable oil, or as needed to fill the fondue pot halfway

emerald SPINACH FONDUE

Frozen spinach is convenient, but not equal to fresh in taste and color. Now that prewashed baby spinach leaves are readily available at most supermarkets, there's no excuse for using frozen. Serve this creamy green fondue with cubes of crusty Italian bread or spicy jalapeño cheese bread; chunks of cooked chicken-apple sausage or grilled beef; cooked prawns or scallops; and lots of fresh vegetables for dunking.

► *Makes about 3 cups; 8 to 10 appetizer servings*

---

6 tablespoons unsalted butter, cut into pieces

⅓ cup chopped shallots

2 tablespoons all-purpose flour

2 cups half-and-half or light cream

2 pounds fresh baby spinach leaves, well rinsed and shaken dry

1 teaspoon salt

½ teaspoon sugar

¼ teaspoon freshly ground black pepper

⅛ teaspoon freshly grated nutmeg

1 package (8 ounces) cream cheese, cut into small pieces

1 tablespoon fresh lemon juice

½ cup freshly grated Parmesan cheese

1 In a nonreactive large saucepan or Dutch oven, melt the butter over medium heat. Add the shallots and cook, stirring occasionally, until softened but not browned, about 2 minutes. Stir in the flour and cook for 1 minute longer. Whisk in 1 cup of the half-and-half.

2 Gradually add the spinach by handfuls, stirring until wilted. Season with the salt, sugar, pepper, and nutmeg. Bring to a boil over medium-high heat and cook, stirring frequently, for 5 minutes. Remove from the heat and let cool slightly.

3 Working in batches, puree the spinach mixture in a food processor or blender until smooth. Return to the pan and place over medium-low heat. Add the remaining 1 cup half-and-half, the cream cheese, and the lemon juice. Cook, stirring frequently, until heated through and blended, about 3 minutes. Stir in the Parmesan cheese.

4 Transfer to a ceramic or enameled cast-iron fondue pot. Regulate the heat, if possible, to keep the fondue warm, not hot.

MUSHROOM STROGANOFF *fondue*

If you're wild about mushrooms, here's the fondue for you. It uses a mix of cultivated and wild, depending upon what's available in your market. Good bread is de rigueur here, because the fondue is so savory, you'll want to mop up as much as possible. Bite-size chunks of cooked beef or chicken, or briefly blanched vegetables like sugar snap peas, tender young green beans, broccoli, or cauliflower are also good for dipping.

► *Makes about 4 cups; 10 to 12 appetizer servings*

---

3 tablespoons unsalted butter

2½ tablespoons all-purpose flour

2 cups beef broth

1 cup crème fraîche or sour cream

1 teaspoon Dijon mustard

1 tablespoon olive oil

1 small onion, chopped

8 ounces fresh white button or cremini mushrooms, coarsely chopped

8 ounces fresh shiitake, chanterelle, and/or morel mushrooms, coarsely chopped

1 teaspoon chopped fresh thyme or ½ teaspoon dried thyme leaves

2 teaspoons fresh lemon juice

Salt and freshly ground black pepper

1 In a medium saucepan, melt 2 tablespoons of the butter over medium heat. Add the flour and cook, stirring, for about 2 minutes without allowing the mixture to color. Increase the heat to medium-high and whisk in the beef broth. Bring to a boil, whisking until smooth and thickened. Reduce the heat to low and simmer, whisking occasionally, for about 3 minutes. Whisk in the crème fraîche and mustard until blended. Remove the sauce from the heat and cover to keep warm.

2 In a large skillet, melt the remaining 1 tablespoon butter in the olive oil over medium-high heat. Add the onion and cook, stirring often, until just golden, 3 to 5 minutes. Add the mushrooms and thyme. Cook, stirring occasionally, until the mushroom liquid is exuded and then evaporates, 5 to 7 minutes. Stir in the lemon juice. Season with ¼ teaspoon each salt and pepper.

3 Reduce the heat to medium-low. Stir the reserved sauce into the mushrooms. Simmer, stirring occasionally, for about 5 minutes to blend the flavors. Season with additional salt and pepper to taste.

4 Transfer to a ceramic fondue pot and serve at once. Regulate the heat under the pot, if possible, so that the fondue remains warm, not hot.

FRIED TORTELLONI *fondue*

St. Louis is known for its breaded fried ravioli. Undoubtedly a great idea, but tortelloni, the larger version of tortellini, are far more interesting—and much easier, because they work well without the bother of breading. Serve with two or three dipping sauces, such as Salsa Verde (page 113), Puttanesca Dipping Sauce (page 126), or your favorite marinara sauce.

► *Makes 8 to 10 appetizer servings*

---

2 packages (9 ounces each) fresh or frozen meat- or cheese-filled tortelloni

3 tablespoons extra-virgin olive oil

About 2 cups peanut or vegetable oil, or enough to fill the fondue pot halfway

1 Cook the tortelloni according to package directions, or until they are just tender but still fairly firm. Drain into a colander and rinse under cold running water. Drain well and pat dry. In a large bowl, toss the tortelloni with the olive oil to coat.

2 Pour the peanut oil into a metal fondue pot, making sure it doesn't fill more than halfway. Set over medium-high heat until it registers 375°F on a deep-frying thermometer.

3 Carefully transfer the pot to a fondue burner with a high flame. Have each guest spear a tortelloni and cook until crisp and lightly golden, about 2 minutes. Give guests each a clean white cloth napkin so they can drain the tortelloni before transferring to their plates, or provide a stack of paper towels.

RUMAKI *fondue*

Here are some retro flavors that are making a big comeback. *Rumaki* is the Hawaiian code word for bacon-wrapped chicken livers or water chestnuts. When preparing rumaki for a fondue, be sure to use thin-sliced bacon: it will cook through relatively quickly. The number of chicken livers to a pound and the number of water chestnuts in a can will often vary, so allow a little wiggle room on quantities. Serve with Apricot-Ginger Dipping Sauce, which follows, as well as another sauce or two, such as Curried Mayonnaise (page 116), Asian Herb Sauce with Lime (page 108), or Ponzu Dipping Sauce (page 109).

Note: For this recipe, you'll need 48 bamboo skewers at least 8 inches long. The skewers should be soaked in a bowl of cold water for at least 30 minutes, then drained and wiped dry before being set on the table.

► *Makes 10 to 12 appetizer servings*

¼ cup soy sauce

2 tablespoons light brown sugar

1 tablespoon dry sherry

8 ounces chicken livers, trimmed and cut into 1-inch pieces

1 can (8 ounces) whole water chestnuts, well drained, halved if larger than 1 inch

1 bunch of scallions, green parts only

16 thin slices of bacon, preferably center-cut (10 to 12 ounces total)

About 2 cups peanut or vegetable oil

1 In a small bowl, combine the soy sauce, brown sugar, and sherry. Pour half of this marinade into another small bowl. Place the chicken livers in one of the bowls and the water chestnuts in the other; toss gently to coat. Cover and refrigerate for 1 hour to marinate. Drain well and pat dry.

2 Cut the scallion greens into 3-inch lengths, or into pieces long enough to wrap around each chicken liver or water chestnut, overlapping slightly. Cut the bacon slices crosswise into thirds.

3 Wrap each chicken liver with a scallion green and then with a bacon slice; secure with a skewer to make each rumaki. Thread only one rumaki on each skewer, keeping it positioned near the top of the skewer to ensure it will be totally submerged in the oil. Blot the rumaki dry with paper towels to absorb any excess moisture. Arrange the skewers on a

chilled platter. Repeat with the water chestnuts and the rest of the scallions and bacon.

4 Heat the oil in a metal fondue pot over medium-high heat until it registers 375°F on a deep-frying thermometer. Transfer the pot to a fondue burner with a high flame. Have each guest select a skewer and cook until the bacon is crisp and the livers are browned outside and pink in the center, 2 to 3 minutes. The water chestnuts will take about 2 minutes, until the bacon is crisp. Have a stack of paper towels nearby so guests can drain the bacon before transferring the rumaki to their plates.

Variation:
Substitute 8 ounces sea scallops, cut into 1-inch pieces, for the chicken livers.

APRICOT-GINGER DIPPING SAUCE

► *Makes 10 to 12 appetizer servings*

---

1 fresh jalapeño pepper, seeded and coarsely chopped

1¼ cups apricot jam

3 tablespoons rice vinegar

2 tablespoons Dijon mustard

1 tablespoon finely grated fresh ginger

2 teaspoons soy sauce

1 Pulse the jalapeño in a food processor to chop finely.

2 Add the jam, vinegar, mustard, ginger, and soy sauce. Process until smooth. Transfer to a small serving bowl and serve at once, or cover and refrigerate for up to 8 hours.

TOMATO-VODKA *fondue*

Everyone loves pasta with vodka sauce, and this recipe turns the dish into a casual fondue—minus the pasta. If you really want to be popular, serve chunks of warm garlic bread for dipping, along with fried polenta cubes, fully cooked cocktail meatballs (which you can make or buy), smoked sausage chunks, ham or grilled chicken cubes, or large cooked shrimp. By the way, save your premium vodka for sipping: With all the spices and seasonings here, a basic brand will be just fine. Vegetables also make great dunkers, especially fried eggplant; oven-roasted zucchini chunks and button mushrooms; and blanched green beans and broccoli.

► *Makes about 4 cups; 10 to 12 appetizer servings*

---

2 tablespoons extra virgin olive oil

1 medium onion, chopped

1 teaspoon salt

2 garlic cloves, minced

½ teaspoon crushed hot red pepper

2 cans (28 ounces each) crushed tomatoes

½ cup vodka

½ cup heavy cream

½ cup freshly grated Parmesan cheese

1½ tablespoons slivered fresh basil

1 In a large nonreactive skillet, heat the oil over medium heat. Add the onion and season with the salt. Cook, stirring occasionally, until softened but not browned, 3 to 5 minutes. Stir in the garlic and hot pepper flakes and cook for 30 seconds longer.

2 Add the crushed tomatoes and vodka, stirring to blend. Reduce the heat to medium-low and simmer uncovered, stirring occasionally, for 1 hour, or until thick. Stir in the cream and cook for 5 minutes longer. Remove from the heat. Add the Parmesan cheese.

3 Using a handheld immersion blender, puree the sauce in the pot until smooth. Alternatively, puree in batches in a blender or food processor. (The fondue can be made to this point up to a day in advance. Reheat before proceeding.)

4 Transfer the vodka sauce to a ceramic fondue pot and sprinkle the basil over the top. Regulate the heat under the pot, if possible, so the fondue remains warm, not hot.

pesto PARTY FONDUE

Pesto may lose its brilliant green color when heated, but its garlicky goodness lives on. Think of this as an herbaceous *bagna cauda*, with fragrant basil standing in for the anchovies. Serve with bread cubes, bite-size slices of fully cooked chicken-apple sausage, cooked fish or shellfish, cherry tomatoes, fennel sticks, or tiny roasted new potatoes for dipping.

► *Makes about 3 cups; 8 to 10 appetizer servings*

---

2 cups basil pesto, purchased or homemade

1 cup extra-virgin olive oil

2 garlic cloves, minced

1 In a small saucepan, combine the pesto, olive oil, and garlic. Cook over low heat, stirring occasionally, just until heated through.

2 Transfer the pesto oil to a fondue pot, preferably ceramic or enameled cast iron, filling no more than halfway. Regulate the heat underneath the pot, if possible, to keep the fondue warm, not hot.

classic BEEF FONDUE

Fondue bourguignonne is a rather fancy name for the simplest and arguably the most delicious fondue. Don't even think about economizing with a cheaper cut of meat; tender beef fillet is the reason this dish has withstood the test of time. Tossing the raw beef cubes in oil before setting them out prevents discoloration and keeps them looking fresh on the platter. For variety, and possibly to stretch the budget, you might like to offer a platter of whole raw mushrooms alongside the meat suggested below. Since they cook so quickly in the hot oil, mushrooms make the perfect "appetizer" to eat while waiting for the beef to cook. Serve with a variety of sauces, such as Béarnaise Mayonnaise (page 114), Madras Curry Mayonnaise (page 116), Spanish Roasted Pepper and Hazelnut Sauce (page 123), Chimichurri Sauce (page 111), Creamy Horseradish Sauce (page 119), and Scandinavian Mustard Sauce (page 120).

If you're offering this as a main course, steamed artichokes make a nice accompaniment, because the leaves can be dipped in the same sauces, and you can nibble on them while the meat is cooking. Be sure to pass a basket of good bread.

► *Makes 6 to 8 main-course or 10 to 12 appetizer servings*

---

2 pounds beef tenderloin, trimmed of all outer fat and membrane, cut into 1-inch cubes

3 tablespoons olive oil

Salt and freshly ground black pepper

About 2 cups peanut or vegetable oil, or enough to fill the fondue pot halfway

1 In a large bowl, toss the beef cubes with the olive oil to coat. Season to taste with salt and pepper. Arrange the beef on a platter or on two or three plates.

2 Pour the peanut oil into a metal fondue pot, making sure it doesn't fill more than halfway. Set over medium-high heat until it registers 375°F on a deep-frying thermometer.

3 Carefully transfer the pot to a fondue burner with a high flame. Spear a piece of beef with a fondue fork or skewer and cook about 2 minutes until rare, or to desired doneness.

CARNITAS *fondue*

In Mexican cuisine, *carnitas* are small cubes of pork, well seasoned and grilled or roasted until crisp. They make a perfect fondue for several reasons: Precooking the meat, as you would for ribs, ensures the pork will be completely done when it's reheated in the hot oil bath. This double cooking crisps the *carnitas* perfectly. And as an appetizer, the little bits lend themselves to any number of dipping sauces, including Chipotle Mayonnaise (page 115), your favorite salsa, and guacamole. To make a meal of this dish, serve the *carnitas* and sauces along with warm soft tortillas and bowls of shredded cheese, thinly sliced scallions, sliced pickled jalapeños, sprigs of cilantro, shredded lettuce, and hot sauce. Rice and beans would not be amiss.

Makes 6 main-course or 10 to 12 appetizer servings

---

3 pounds boneless pork butt or shoulder

1 teaspoon dried oregano

1 teaspoon salt

¾ teaspoon freshly ground black pepper

½ teaspoon ground cumin

4 garlic cloves, crushed with the flat side of a knife

1 bay leaf

About 2 cups peanut oil, or enough to fill the fondue pot halfway

Lime wedges, for serving

1 Trim the outer fat off the pork and cut the meat into 1-inch cubes.

2 In a medium bowl, mix together the oregano, salt, pepper, and cumin. Add the pork cubes and toss to coat lightly. Let stand for 10 to 20 minutes.

3 Place the meat in a large deep skillet or Dutch oven, preferably in a single layer. Add enough cold water to just barely cover. Add the garlic and bay leaf and bring to a boil over high heat. Reduce the heat to medium-low and simmer, uncovered, stirring occasionally, until the liquid evaporates and the meat begins to sizzle in its own fat, 50 minutes to 1 hour. (The recipe can be made to this point up to a day ahead. Let return to room temperature before proceeding.) Arrange the *carnitas* on a platter.

(continued)

4 Pour the peanut oil into a metal fondue pot, making sure it doesn't fill more than halfway. Set over medium-high heat until it registers 375°F on a deep-frying thermometer.

5 Carefully transfer the pot to a fondue burner with a high flame. Have each guest spear a cube of pork and cook until crisp and brown, 2 to 3 minutes. Give guests each a clean cloth napkin so they can drain the *carnitas* before transferring to their plates, or provide a stack of paper towels. Serve with lime wedges to squeeze over the meat, as well as an assortment of dipping sauces.

AMERICAN HOT-POT FONDUE *with spicy barbecue broth*

This fondue offers an assortment of meats: beef, pork, and chicken. The cooking liquid is an easy doctored-up broth flavored with aromatics and bottled barbecue sauce. (For this dish, avoid hickory smoke sauce, which can be overpowering.) Along with the beef, pork, and chicken for dunking, offer a colorful selection of vegetables, such as sweet bell peppers, wedges of sweet onion, halved roasted new potatoes, canned baby whole corn, trimmed green beans, and broccoli florets. Some of the same barbecue sauce used to flavor the broth can also be presented as a dipping sauce, along with Chipotle Mayonnaise (page 115) and Creamy Horseradish Sauce (page119).

Makes 4 to 6 main-course or 10 to 12 appetizer servings

---

4 cups chicken or beef broth

1½ cups barbecue sauce

1 tablespoon prepared white horseradish

1 tablespoon brown sugar

1 tablespoon cider vinegar

1 medium onion, coarsely chopped

3 garlic cloves, crushed with the flat side of a knife

½ teaspoon hot pepper sauce

12 ounces beef tenderloin, trimmed of any outer fat and membrane

12 ounces pork tenderloin, trimmed of any outer fat and membrane

1 In a medium nonreactive saucepan, bring the broth and ½ cup of water to a boil over high heat. Reduce the heat to medium-low. Whisk in the barbecue sauce, horseradish, brown sugar, and vinegar. Stir in the onion, garlic, and hot sauce. Simmer, uncovered, for 20 minutes. Strain the broth through a sieve, pressing down on the solids to release as much liquid as possible. Return the broth to the same pot and set aside, covered to keep warm.

2 While the broth is simmering, put the beef and pork in the freezer so it will be easier to slice. Cut the chicken crosswise on the diagonal into thin slices. When the beef and pork are firm, cut them against the grain into slices about ⅛ inch thick. Arrange the meats on three separate chilled platters.

(continued)

8 ounces skinless, boneless chicken breasts, trimmed of any fat or tendons

3 Pour enough hot broth into a metal fondue pot to reach no more than halfway up the sides, then carefully set the pot over a high flame. Keep the remaining broth warm in the kitchen so you can replenish the fondue pot as needed.

4 Have each guest spear a piece of meat, chicken, or vegetable with a fondue fork or skewer. Cook in the warm broth until the chicken is white throughout, the meats are cooked to the desired doneness, and the vegetables are hot and crisp-tender.

ROSEMARY LAMB *spiedini*

Consider this fondue when you have access to a good supply of fresh rosemary, a little time on your hands, and the desire to wow your guests. *Spiedini* is Italian for "skewers." Of course, the lamb can be threaded onto bamboo sticks, but rosemary branches make a spectacular—and fragrant—presentation. Serve with at least three dipping sauces, such as Piquant Mint Sauce (page 112), Chipotle Mayonnaise (page 115), Salsa Verde (page 113), or Mint Pesto-Yogurt Sauce (page 122).

Note: For this dish, you'll need 36 sturdy rosemary stems or bamboo skewers at least 8 inches long. Leaving about 1 inch of the rosemary at the tip, run your fingers down the stem to remove the leaves. Before threading the meat and peppers on the rosemary, soak the stems (or bamboo skewers) in water for about 30 minutes to prevent them from burning in the hot oil. Remember to dry them thoroughly, as wet sticks will cause the hot oil to sputter. If the rosemary stems are short, be sure to put a few pairs of metal tongs on the table and encourage guests to share them.

► *Makes 4 to 5 main-course or 10 to 12 appetizer servings*

1½ tablespoons fresh lemon juice

2 teaspoons finely chopped fresh rosemary or 1 teaspoon dried, crumbled

2 garlic cloves, crushed through a press

½ teaspoon salt

¼ teaspoon freshly ground black pepper

3½ tablespoons extra-virgin olive oil

2 pounds boneless leg of lamb, trimmed of fat and membranes, cut into 1-inch cubes

1 In a large bowl, combine the lemon juice, rosemary, garlic, salt, and pepper. Whisk in the olive oil until the marinade is well blended. Add the lamb and toss gently to coat. Cover with plastic wrap and let stand up for to 2 hours at room temperature, tossing once or twice. Drain and discard any remaining marinade.

2 Thread 1 lamb cube and 1 bell pepper square onto each rosemary stem or skewer. Arrange the spiedini on a platter in a circular pattern with the stem ends facing out.

3 Pour the peanut oil into a metal fondue pot, making sure not to fill it more than halfway. Set over medium-high heat until it registers 375°F on a deep-frying thermometer.

2 or 3 large red bell peppers, cut into 1-inch squares

About 2 cups peanut or vegetable oil, or enough to fill the fondue pot halfway

4 Transfer the pot to a fondue burner with a high flame. Have each guest cook the spiedini for about 2 minutes for medium-rare, or to desired doneness.

thai-flavored SHELLFISH FONDUE

A mix of shrimp, oysters, and scallops stars in this subtle Thai-inspired fondue, perfumed with lemon grass and ginger. You can, if you prefer, use all shrimp, or substitute clams on the half-shell for the shucked oysters. In addition to the seafood, offer a generous platter of fresh vegetables for cooking in the broth: think snow peas or sugar snap peas, red bell pepper strips, 2-inch lengths of scallion, small shiitake or button mushroom caps, or broccoli florets. Offer three sauces for dipping, such as Spicy Orange-Ginger Dipping Sauce (page 117), Zesty Asian-Style Cocktail Sauce (page 125), Ponzu Dipping Sauce (page 109), or Asian Herb Sauce with Lime (page 108). As a main course offering, rice or Asian noodles would not be amiss.

► *Makes 4 to 6 main-course or 10 to 12 appetizer servings*

---

3 cups (24 ounces) bottled clam juice

2 tablespoons Asian fish sauce (*nam pla* or *nuoc nam*)

Finely grated zest and juice of 1 lime

4 whole scallions, cut into 2-inch pieces

1 stalk of fresh lemongrass, tough outer leaves removed, inner white core cut into 1-inch pieces and crushed with the flat side of a knife

1 piece of fresh ginger 1½ inches long, peeled and coarsely chopped

1 tablespoon light brown sugar

1 In a large saucepan, combine the clam juice, fish sauce, lime zest and juice, scallions, lemongrass, ginger, brown sugar, cilantro, jalapeño, garlic, and peppercorns. Add 3 cups of water. Bring to a boil over high heat. Remove from the heat and let stand for 30 minutes to develop the flavors.

2 Strain the broth through a sieve, pressing down gently on the solids to extract as much liquid as possible. Return the broth to the same saucepan and cook over low heat until heated through. (The broth can be prepared up to 8 hours in advance and refrigerated. Reheat before using.)

3 On a large chilled platter, arrange the shrimp, oysters, and scallops. (If assembling in advance, cover with plastic wrap and refrigerate for up to 8 hours.)

6 cilantro stems without leaves

1 fresh jalapeño pepper, halved and seeded

1 large garlic clove, crushed with the flat side of a knife

¼ teaspoon whole black peppercorns

1 pound large shrimp, peeled and deveined

24 to 36 oysters, shucked and drained

12 ounces sea scallops, halved crosswise

4 Pour enough hot broth into a metal fondue pot to reach no more than halfway up the sides; then carefully set the pot over a high flame. Keep the remaining broth warm in the kitchen so you can replenish the fondue pot as needed.

5 Have each guest lift a piece of shellfish or vegetable with chopsticks or spear with a fondue fork. Cook in the hot broth until the vegetables are crisp-tender and the seafood is opaque throughout, 30 seconds to 3 minutes.

tabletop FISH FRY

Fried fish need not be battered in order to be delicious. Here a light, citrus-laced marinade adds all the interest. When serving seafood at a fondue party, arrange the raw fish artistically on a large chilled platter to keep it cool; crushed ice is both practical and dramatic if you have it on hand. Tangy Tartar Sauce (page 118), is an expected pairing. For fun serve a couple of other sauces as well, such as Zesty Asian-Style Cocktail Sauce (page 125) or Spicy Orange-Ginger Dipping Sauce (page 117).

► *Makes 4 to 6 main-course or 10 to 12 appetizer servings*

1/3 cup soy sauce

1/3 cup dry vermouth

1/4 cup fresh lime juice

1 tablespoon Asian sesame oil

4 thin slices of fresh ginger, crushed with the flat side of a knife

12 ounces large shrimp, shelled and deveined

8 ounces skinless, boneless firm-fleshed fish, such as tuna or swordfish, cut into 1-inch cubes

8 ounces sea scallops

8 ounces cleaned squid (calamari), sacs cut into 3/8-inch-thick rings, tentacles halved lengthwise

About 2 cups peanut or vegetable oil, or enough to fill the fondue pot halfway

Lime wedges, for serving

1 In a medium bowl, whisk together the soy sauce, vermouth, lime juice, and sesame oil to make a marinade.

2 Put the shrimp in a 1-gallon zipper-seal plastic bag. Add 1 slice of crushed ginger and about 3 1/2 tablespoons of the marinade. Seal the bag securely and shake gently to distribute the marinade. Repeat with the fish, scallops, and squid each in separate bags. Refrigerate for 1 hour.

3 Drain the shrimp, fish, scallops, and squid, keeping each separate. Pat them dry with paper towels. Arrange on a well-chilled platter.

4 Pour the peanut oil into a metal fondue pot, making sure not to fill it more than halfway. Set over medium-high heat until it registers 375°F on a deep-frying thermometer.

5 Carefully transfer the pot to a fondue burner with a high flame. Have each guest spear a piece of seafood and cook until just opaque throughout, 1 to 3 minutes. Serve with a bowl of lime wedges for squeezing over the seafood after it is cooked.

DESSERT *fondues*

CHOCOLATE MIDNIGHT *fondue*

Here's the "little black dress" of chocolate fondues: basic, elegant, and adaptable. Whether you prefer the intensity of dark bittersweet or the slightly sweeter semisweet, choose a good-quality chocolate you would enjoy eating out of hand. Cognac is the classic flavoring, but dark rum, bourbon, Kahlúa, Grand Marnier, or just about any liqueur works equally well. If you prefer to forgo the alcohol altogether, substitute an equal amount of one of the bottled syrups used for flavoring coffee drinks, or 1 teaspoon vanilla, almond, or orange extract. Pull out all the stops when it comes to dipping here. Offer a colorful assortment of fresh and dried fruits—keeping in mind that strawberries are usually the hands-down favorite. Also think marshmallows, sugar or nut cookies, donut holes, pretzels, small squares of waffle, frozen bits of cheesecake, and bite-size cubes of angel food or pound cake.

► *Makes about 2½ cups; 8 to 10 servings*

---

1 cup heavy cream

Dash of salt

1 pound bittersweet and/or semisweet chocolate, chopped

2 tablespoons cognac or brandy

1 In a medium saucepan, heat the cream and salt over low heat until hot but not boiling. Gradually stir in the chocolate, letting each addition melt before adding more. Stir in the cognac.

2 Transfer to a ceramic fondue pot and set over a low flame. Regulate the flame under the fondue to keep it as low as possible. If it begins to boil, turn off the heat.

Variations:

CHOCOLATE ALMOND FONDUE: Substitute amaretto for the cognac. Serve with fresh or dried apricots, and small bowls of chopped toasted almonds on the side to roll the chocolate-coated bites in.

CHOCOLATE FONDUE À L'ORANGE: Substitute Grand Marnier, Cointreau,

(continued)

Triple Sec, or other orange-flavored liqueur for the cognac.

CHOCOLATE-HAZELNUT FONDUE: Substitute Frangelico or other hazelnut liqueur for the cognac. For added richness, stir in 3 tablespoons chocolate-hazelnut spread, such as Nutella, until melted and smooth.

CHOCOLATE MACCHIATO FONDUE: Before adding the chocolate, add 1 teaspoon of instant espresso powder to the warm cream and stir until dissolved. Substitute a coffee liqueur, such as Kahlúa, for the cognac.

CHOCOLATE–PIÑA COLADA FONDUE: Substitute dark rum and 1/2 teaspoon coconut extract for the cognac. Serve with fresh or dried pineapple chunks, and small bowls of sweetened flaked coconut on the side to roll the chocolate-coated bites in.

CHOCOLATE RAZZLE-DAZZLE FONDUE: Substitute framboise (raspberry eau-de-vie) or Chambord (black raspberry liqueur) for the cognac, and stir in 1 cup (6 ounces) fresh raspberries.

CHOCOLATE VOODOO FONDUE: Substitute crème de banana for the cognac. Serve banana chips and fresh banana chunks for dipping.

DARK CHOCOLATE–MINT FONDUE: Substitute crème de menthe or a chocolate-peppermint liqueur, such as Vandermint for the cognac.

IRISH DREAM FONDUE: Substitute 1 tablespoon Irish whiskey and 2 tablespoons Baileys or other Irish cream liqueur for the cognac.

BLACK FOREST *fondue*

This recipe proves it takes only a few ingredients—and a few minutes— to make a luscious dessert. For a change of pace, vary the jam and liqueur. Try bitter orange marmalade with Grand Marnier, apricot jam with amaretto, or seedless raspberry jam with Chambord. Serve with cubes of vanilla or chocolate pound cake, angel food cake, meringue cookies, shortbread cookies, crisp ladyfingers, marshmallows, or sliced apples or pears.

► *Makes about 4 cups; 10 to 12 servings*

---

2 cups heavy cream

1 pound bittersweet chocolate, chopped

⅓ cup sour cherry jam or other cherry preserves, chopped

2 tablespoons kirsch or cherry liqueur, such as Cherry Heering (optional)

Dash of salt

1 In a medium saucepan, warm the cream over medium-low heat, watching carefully, until bubbles appear around the edge of the pan. Remove from the heat and gradually stir in the chocolate, letting each addition melt before adding more. Stir in the jam, kirsch, and salt.

2 Transfer to a ceramic fondue pot. Regulate the flame under the fondue to keep it as low as possible. If it begins to boil, turn off the heat.

almost-instant

CHOCOLATE BUTTERSCOTCH FONDUE

When there are only a few ingredients in a recipe, they must be of the best quality. My friend Barb Shenson, who shared this recipe, recommends you skip the inexpensive generic brands of ice cream topping and go for a butterscotch sauce with body and rich flavor. You may want to add a tablespoon or two of dark rum, bourbon, or brandy; it will enhance the flavor. For dipping, include platters of your favorite shortbread cookies, madeleines, small squares of angel food cake, brownies, frozen cheesecake, dried apricots, or fresh strawberries and apple slices.

► *Makes about 3½ cups; 8 to 10 servings*

1½ cups heavy cream

1 jar (16 to 17 ounces) caramel or butterscotch sauce, preferably Mrs. Richardson's Butterscotch Caramel Sauce

Dash of salt

18 ounces bittersweet chocolate, chopped

1 In a medium saucepan, combine the cream, caramel sauce, and salt. Warm over low heat, whisking frequently, until melted and smooth. Gradually stir in the chocolate, letting each addition melt before adding more.

2 Transfer to a ceramic or enameled cast-iron fondue pot and set over a low flame. Regulate the heat under the fondue to keep it as low as possible. If it begins to boil, turn off the heat.

CHOCOLATE CHEESECAKE *fondue*

Adding cream cheese to a simple chocolate fondue creates just the right amount of body to ensure the slick sweet adheres to your cake or fruit without being too thick or heavy. The slight tang is pleasing and tastes very much like a chocolate cheesecake filling. Cookbook author and friend Susan Wyler suggests serving her creation with toasted pound cake cubes, ladyfingers, and/or cut up fruit for dipping. Mango, strawberries, pineapple, dried orange peel, and dried apricots are especially good. And since we're talking cheesecake here, it seems only right to acknowledge that classic crust by offering graham crackers to dip as well.

► *Makes about 2 cups; 6 to 8 servings*

---

1 cup heavy cream

3 tablespoons confectioners' sugar

4 ounces cream cheese, at room temperature

12 ounces semisweet chocolate, coarsely chopped

1 teaspoon vanilla extract

1 In a small heavy saucepan, whisk together the cream and confectioners' sugar. Warm over medium-low heat, stirring, until bubbles appear around the edge of the pan.

2 Add the cream cheese and continue to cook, stirring often, until the cheese is melted and the cream is smooth.

3 Put the chopped chocolate in a ceramic fondue pot. Pour in the hot cream and whisk until the chocolate is melted. Whisk in the vanilla. Keep warm over a low flame for dipping. Do not allow it to boil.

MEXICAN HOT CHOCOLATE *fondue*

Here smooth, dark chocolate is combined with some typical Mexican flavors, including the smoky kick of chipotle chile, just as in Aztec times. Strawberries, pineapple, and mango make excellent dippers, as do banana bread and cinnamon donut holes. (Some might even opt for the comfort of chocolate chip cookies.) Cinnamon sticks infuse the cream with a subtle yet distinctive flavor, but if you have none on hand, simply add 1 teaspoon of ground cinnamon along with the espresso and chile powders.

► *Makes about 3 cups; 8 to 10 servings*

- 1 cup heavy cream
- 1 cup whole milk
- 3 cinnamon sticks
- 1 pound semisweet chocolate, chopped
- 1 teaspoon instant espresso powder
- 1 teaspoon ground chipotle chile
- ½ teaspoon vanilla extract

1 In a medium saucepan, combine the cream, milk, and cinnamon sticks. Cook over medium-low heat, watching carefully, until small bubbles appear around the edges of the pan. Reduce the heat to low and cook for 5 minutes longer. Remove and discard the cinnamon sticks.

2 Gradually add the chocolate to the cinnamon-infused cream mixture and cook, stirring, until melted and smooth. Stir in the espresso powder, chipotle powder, and vanilla. Continue cooking and stirring over low heat for 1 minute longer.

3 Transfer to a ceramic fondue pot and set over a low flame. Regulate the heat, if possible, to keep the fondue warm, not hot. If it begins to boil, turn off the heat.

CHOCOLATE-COCONUT *fondue*

If you like a certain chocolate-covered coconut cream candy bar (which has a toasted almond positioned on top), chances are you'll love this fondue. Cream of coconut, the sweetened kind used for exotic drinks, provides the rich coconut flavor here. Do not substitute unsweetened coconut milk. Serve with fresh strawberries, chunks of mango or banana; seedless orange or tangerine segments; bite-size pieces of angel food cake; macaroons; or crunchy almond biscotti.

► *Makes about 3 cups; 8 to 10 servings*

1¼ cups sweetened cream of coconut, such as Coco Reál or Coco Lopez

½ cup heavy cream

8 ounces bittersweet chocolate, chopped

1 to 2 tablespoons sweetened flaked coconut

1 In a medium saucepan, heat the cream of coconut and heavy cream over medium-low heat, watching carefully, until heated through. Gradually add the chocolate and cook, stirring, until melted and smooth.

2 Transfer to a ceramic fondue pot and sprinkle the shredded coconut over the top as garnish. Regulate the heat, if possible, to keep the fondue warm, not hot. If it begins to boil, turn off the heat.

TOBLERONE SWISS CHOCOLATE *fondue*

Toblerone is a fine-quality Swiss candy bar that blends chocolate with honey and chopped almonds. It is reputed to have played a role in the first chocolate fondue to appear in a New York City restaurant. In 1964, a chef named Konrad Egli, working at the Chalet Suisse restaurant, offered melted Toblerone bars with fruit for dipping to lure more of the clientele into ordering dessert. Needless to say, the idea took off. Serve this fondue with crisp ladyfingers, almond biscotti, bite-size chunks of angel food cake, orange or tangerine sections, dried apricots, dried or fresh figs, strawberries, or bananas. If by some chance there is any leftover fondue, it can be refrigerated until firm and rolled into balls, to serve as truffles.

► *Makes about 2 cups; 6 to 8 servings*

¾ cup heavy cream

6 bars (3½ ounces each) milk chocolate or semisweet Toblerone, broken into pieces

2 tablespoons cognac

1 In a medium saucepan, heat the cream over low heat until hot but not boiling. Gradually stir in the chocolate, letting each addition melt before adding more. Stir in the cognac.

2 Transfer the chocolate mixture to a ceramic fondue pot and set over a low flame. Regulate the heat, if possible, to keep the fondue warm, not hot. If it begins to boil, turn off the heat.

MINTED MILK CHOCOLATE *fondue*

Chocolate-covered mint candies provide the perfect proportion of sweet dark chocolate to refreshing hint of mint in this easy dessert dip. Strawberries, banana chunks, plain cookies, and bits of cake are naturals for dunking, but don't overlook the decadent delight of other treats, such as pretzels, marshmallows, and even creme-filled chocolate sandwich cookies.

► *Makes about 2½ cups; 6 to 8 servings*

⅔ cup heavy cream

¼ cup whole milk

10 small, round (1½-inch) chocolate-covered peppermint candies, such as York Peppermint Patties, chopped

8 ounces milk chocolate, chopped

1 to 2 tablespoons chocolate-peppermint liqueur, such as Vandermint, or ½ teaspoon peppermint extract

1 In a medium saucepan, combine the cream and milk. Cook over medium-low heat, watching carefully, just until heated through. Add the peppermint patties and cook, stirring, until mostly melted. Gradually add the milk chocolate and cook, stirring constantly, until melted and smooth. Stir in the liqueur or peppermint extract.

2 Transfer to a ceramic fondue pot and set over a low flame. Regulate the heat, if possible, to keep the fondue warm, not hot. If it begins to boil, turn off the heat.

BANANAS FOSTER *fondue*

When paired with white chocolate, the New Orleans dessert made famous by Brennan's restaurant makes a memorable fondue. Serve with fresh strawberries or pineapple chunks; crêpes, rolled and cut into 1-inch pieces; warm squares of waffle, chocolate wafers, madeleines, or bite-size pieces of pound cake.

► *Makes about 4 cups; 10 to 12 servings*

---

1 pound white chocolate, chopped

4 tablespoons unsalted butter, cut into pieces

1 cup packed brown sugar

½ cup dark rum

½ teaspoon ground cinnamon

2 firm but ripe bananas, halved and thinly sliced or chopped

1 to 2 tablespoons crème de banana liqueur (optional)

1 In a double boiler or a large heatproof bowl placed over a pan of barely simmering water, melt the white chocolate, stirring occasionally, until smooth.

2 In a large saucepan, combine the butter, brown sugar, rum, and cinnamon. Cook over medium-low heat, stirring occasionally, until the sugar has melted and the mixture is heated through. Gradually stir in the melted white chocolate. Add the bananas, banana liqueur, and 2 tablespoons of water.

3 Transfer to a ceramic fondue pot and set over low heat. Regulate the flame under the fondue to keep it as low as possible. If it begins to boil, turn off the heat.

WHITE CHOCOLATE–PEACH *fondue*

Peaches and cream never had it so good. Silky honey adds both flavor and body to this fondue, and complements the richness of the peaches. Although this may look like a lot of bourbon to some, most of the alcohol cooks away, and it prevents the fondue from being too sweet.

► *Makes about 4 cups; 10 to 12 servings*

1½ cups heavy cream

½ cup honey

1 cup peeled and finely chopped fresh or thawed frozen peaches

¼ cup bourbon

1 pound white chocolate, chopped

1 In a medium saucepan, combine the cream and honey. Cook over medium heat, stirring until smooth, 3 to 5 minutes. Stir in the peaches and the bourbon and cook for 5 minutes longer, or until heated through.

2 Put the white chocolate into a ceramic fondue pot. Pour in the hot peach mixture and whisk until the chocolate is melted. Keep warm over a low flame for dipping. If the fondue begins to boil, turn off the heat.

GINGERED WHITE CHOCOLATE *fondue*

A triple dose of ginger—candied, ground, and fresh—lends extra sophistication to this snowy white fondue. Serve with bite-size squares of angel food cake, pineapple chunks, dried apricots, Chinese fortune cookies, and—of course—gingersnaps. When buying white chocolate, be sure the label lists cocoa butter as a major ingredient; confectionery coating, also called summer coating, will not work for fondue.

► *Makes about 3 cups; 8 to 10 servings*

---

2 cups heavy cream

3 tablespoons finely chopped crystallized ginger

1½ tablespoons ground ginger

1 teaspoon finely grated fresh ginger

1 pound white chocolate, chopped

1 In a medium saucepan, combine the cream, 2 tablespoons of the crystallized ginger, the ground ginger, and the fresh ginger. Cook over medium heat, watching to make sure it doesn't bubble up, until heated through.

2 Put the white chocolate in a ceramic fondue pot. Pour in the hot cream and whisk until the chocolate is melted. Sprinkle the remaining 1 tablespoon crystallized ginger over the top. Keep warm over a low flame for dipping. If it begins to boil, turn off the heat.

Variation:

MARBLED CHOCOLATE FONDUE

Omit the ginger. In a small heatproof bowl set over a pan of barely simmering water, melt 4 ounces of bittersweet chocolate with 2 teaspoons of butter until melted and smooth. Transfer the white chocolate mixture to a fondue pot. Pipe or spoon concentric circles (or another decorative design) of the dark chocolate mixture over the top and swirl through with a thin wooden skewer.

VERY BERRY *fondue*

Ripe fresh berries are naturally the best choice for this pure fruit fondue. Out of season, frozen berries can still make a memorable sweet-tart dessert, but be sure to choose unsweetened, individually quick-frozen berries. For dipping, offer shortbread or crisp gingerbread cookies, bite-size cubes of pound cake; chocolate or hazelnut biscotti; apple or nectarine wedges; or chilled cubes of mild cheese, such as Brie or Havarti.

► *Makes about 2¾ cups; 6 to 8 servings*

---

4 cups (two 1-pint baskets) fresh whole strawberries, hulled, or 1 package (12 ounces) frozen unsweetened strawberries, thawed

3 cups (about 18 ounces) fresh raspberries or 1 package (12 ounces) frozen unsweetened raspberries, thawed

½ cup unsweetened apple juice

¼ cup sugar

2 tablespoons cornstarch

2 tablespoons black raspberry liqueur, such as Chambord

½ pint (6 ounces) fresh blueberries or 1 cup frozen unsweetened blueberries, thawed

1 Puree the strawberries and raspberries in a food processor until smooth, working in batches, if necessary. Strain the puree through a sieve to remove the seeds, pressing and working the bits in the sieve to extract as much of the fruit and juice as possible.

2 Place the berry puree in a medium nonreactive saucepan. Stir in the apple juice and sugar.

3 In a small bowl, whisk the cornstarch with the liqueur until completely blended. Whisk into the berry puree and bring to a boil over medium heat, stirring. Reduce the heat to low and simmer, stirring frequently, until the puree is slightly thickened, about 3 minutes. Add the blueberries and cook until just heated through, about 3 minutes longer. Do not let the berries burst.

4 Transfer to a ceramic fondue pot set over a low flame.

CARAMEL FONDUE *with fleur de sel*

When making caramel at home, be sure to purchase sugar labeled "pure cane sugar." For the sake of economy, some less expensive store brands periodically blend cane sugar with beet sugar. This doesn't affect the flavor, but it can make caramelizing the sugar extremely difficult, if not impossible. Just a tiny garnish of sea salt gives a surprising lift and relieves the sticky sweetness of the caramel. Serve this dessert fondue with cold, crisp wedges of tart apple, chunks of bananas, or any seasonal fruit. And don't forget chewy brownies, cut into small squares.

Makes about 2½ cups; 6 to 8 servings

---

1 cup pure cane sugar

2⅔ cups heavy cream, heated

2 tablespoons unsalted butter, cut into bits

1 teaspoon vanilla extract

¼ teaspoon *fleur de sel* or other coarse salt

1 In a medium saucepan, combine the sugar and ¼ cup of water. Cook over medium-low heat, stirring, until the sugar dissolves. Increase the heat to medium and cook without stirring, swirling the pan and occasionally brushing down the sides with a wet pastry brush to remove any sugar crystals, until the mixture turns a medium-dark amber, about 3 minutes.

2 Carefully pour in the warm cream, stirring until the caramel is dissolved and smooth. (The cream will bubble up.) Increase the heat to medium-high and boil, stirring occasionally, until the caramel cream is smooth and thick enough to coat the back of a spoon, about 10 minutes. Remove from the heat and stir in the butter and vanilla.

3 Pour the hot caramel into a ceramic or enameled cast-iron fondue pot and sprinkle the *fleur de sel* over the top. Regulate the heat, if possible, to keep the fondue warm, not hot.

CHOCOLATE CHIP *celebration fondue*

Who needs birthday cake? Let the budding gourmet in your family celebrate in style over a pot of barely warm molten chocolate. So sophisticated, yet so easy on mom. Serve with the celebrant's favorite cookies or cubes of angel food or pound cake for dunking, along with pretzels, dried apricots, and a colorful array of fresh fruit, such as pineapple and banana chunks, orange segments, seedless grapes, and whole strawberries.

► *Makes about 3½ cups; 10 to 12 servings*

---

1 cup whole milk

3½ cups (21 ounces) semisweet chocolate chips

1 tablespoon vanilla extract

Dash of salt

1 In a medium saucepan, warm the milk over medium-low heat, watching carefully, until heated through. Reduce the heat to low and gradually whisk in the chocolate chips, letting each addition melt before adding more. Whisk in the vanilla and salt.

2 Transfer to a ceramic fondue pot and set over a low flame. Regulate the heat under the fondue to keep it as low as possible. If it begins to boil, turn off the heat.

DULCE DE LECHE *fondue*

This Latin-inspired milk caramel fondue is made the old-fashioned way, with real sugar and cream instead of canned milk, and with a healthy dose of rum. Use it for dunking strawberries, melon, banana or pineapple chunks, mango, apple, store-bought pirouette cookies, or bite-size cubes of pound cake or semifrozen banana nut bread.

► *Makes about 2 cups; 6 to 8 servings*

---

1 cup sugar

2 cups heavy cream, heated

¼ cup dark rum or 2 teaspoons vanilla extract

Dash of salt

1 In a medium saucepan, combine the sugar and ¼ cup of water. Cook over medium-low heat, stirring, until the sugar dissolves. Increase the heat to medium and cook without stirring, swirling the pan and occasionally brushing down the sides with a wet pastry brush to remove any sugar crystals, until the syrup turns a medium-dark amber, about 3 minutes.

2 Carefully pour in the warm cream, stirring until the caramel is dissolved and smooth. (The cream will bubble up.) Stir in the rum and salt. Increase the heat to medium-high and boil, stirring occasionally, until the caramel cream, or *dulce de leche,* is smooth and thick enough to coat the back of a spoon, about 10 minutes.

3 Carefully transfer to a ceramic or enameled cast-iron fondue pot. Regulate the heat under the pot, if possible, so that the fondue remains warm, not hot.

PEANUT BUTTER FONDUE
with chocolate swirls

For those who love peanut butter, what better idea than to pair it with chocolate? To prevent separating, use a standard commercial peanut butter. Creamy is recommended for a smooth coating. Even though there is salt in the peanut butter, a little extra is added to balance the sweetness of the chocolate. Because this fondue is a little thicker than some, sturdier dippers are a good idea: try chewy brownies cut into small squares, shortbread cookies, pretzel sticks, biscotti, banana chunks, apple wedges, and orange segments.

► *Makes about 3 cups; 8 to 10 servings*

---

1 cup heavy cream

3 tablespoons light brown sugar

⅛ teaspoon salt

2 cups creamy peanut butter

1 teaspoon vanilla extract

2 ounces semisweet or milk chocolate, finely chopped

1 In a medium saucepan, stir the cream, brown sugar, and salt over medium heat until the sugar has melted and the cream is hot but not boiling. Gradually stir in the peanut butter until melted and smooth. Stir in the vanilla.

2 Transfer to a ceramic fondue pot and set over a low flame. Scatter the chocolate over the top and let stand for about 1 minute to allow it to soften. Using a fondue fork or a skewer, swirl the melted chocolate over the top of the fondue. Regulate the heat, if possible, to keep the fondue warm, not hot.

SPICED ORANGE-CRANBERRY *fondue*

This fondue has all the fragrant appeal of mulled wine and the irresistible flavor of tart-sweet cranberries. Make it part of your holiday dessert buffet, serving an array of dippers such as orange segments, apple or pear wedges, madeleines, cubes of fruit cake, tiny store-bought cream puffs, ginger snaps or gingerbread, glacéed pineapple slices, and bite-size cubes of panettone.

► *Makes about 3 cups; 8 to 10 servings*

1½ cups cabernet sauvignon or other dry red wine

1½ cups sugar

½ cup orange juice

1 cinnamon stick (about 3 inches long)

3 cups (12 ounces) fresh or frozen cranberries

2 tablespoons Grand Marnier or other orange-flavored liqueur

1 tablespoon cornstarch

1 In a medium nonreactive saucepan, combine the wine, sugar, orange juice, and cinnamon stick. Bring to a boil over medium-high heat, stirring to dissolve the sugar. Add the cranberries.

2 In a small bowl, whisk the liqueur with the cornstarch until completely blended. Stir into the cranberry mixture and cook over medium heat until the liquid reaches a boil. Reduce the heat to medium-low and simmer, stirring frequently, until the fondue is slightly thickened, about 3 minutes. Discard the cinnamon stick.

3 Transfer the fondue to a ceramic fondue pot set over a low flame. Regulate the heat, if possible, to keep the fondue warm, not hot.

RASPBERRY CREAM *fondue*

Sweet-tart, intense, and pleasingly acidic, raspberries have a fabulous potent flavor that can carry a creamy fondue. Removing the seeds from the berries is the only work required here, but it's well worth the small effort. Accompany the fondue with plain or lemon shortbread cookies, crisp meringue cookies, brownie bites, madeleines, angel food or pound cake cubes, and just about any fresh fruit that catches your eye at the market.

► *Makes about 2¼ cups; 6 to 8 servings*

---

2 packages (10 ounces each) frozen raspberries in syrup, thawed

⅓ cup confectioners' sugar

1 cup heavy cream

2 tablespoons framboise or orange-flavored liqueur

2 teaspoons fresh lemon juice

1 In a food processor or blender, combine the raspberries and confectioners' sugar. Puree until smooth. Strain the raspberry puree through a fine sieve into a bowl, pressing hard on the seeds to force through as much fruit and juice as possible.

2 In a medium nonreactive saucepan, heat the cream over medium-high heat, watching carefully, just until bubbles form around the edges. Reduce the heat to medium-low and stir in the raspberry puree, framboise, and lemon juice.

3 Transfer to a ceramic fondue pot set over a low flame. Regulate the heat, if possible, to keep the fondue warm, not hot.

S'MORE *fondue*

You don't have to be a scout or a kid to love the classic combination of chocolate and marshmallows that keeps everyone asking for more. What to dip? Graham crackers and marshmallows, of course, along with bananas, strawberries, apples, and pineapple chunks.

► *Makes about 3 cups; 8 to 10 servings*

½ cup whole milk

5 tablespoons butter, cut into pieces

24 large marshmallows

Dash of salt

1½ cups (9 ounces) semi-sweet chocolate chips

1 In a heavy medium saucepan, combine the milk, butter, half of the marshmallows, and the salt. Cook over medium-low heat, whisking frequently, until the butter and marshmallows are melted and smooth, 3 to 5 minutes.

2 Add the remaining marshmallows and whisk until melted and well blended. Reduce the heat to low and gradually stir in the chocolate chips, letting each addition melt before adding more.

3 Transfer to a ceramic fondue pot and set over a low flame. Regulate the heat, if possible, to keep the fondue warm, not hot.

SWEET WINE AND CHEESE *fondue*

Wine with cheese, fruit and cheese for dessert—these traditional pairings are captured in this grown-up dessert fondue, inspired by a recipe that once appeared in *Sunset* magazine. A sweet, full-flavored wine forms the base; Essensia, an orange muscat from Quady Winery in California, or an Italian *vin santo*, would be ideal. The wine will be drastically reduced to a syrup, so a French Sauterne is probably not the best choice, both because of the cost and because it would be a waste not to drink it. Serve this fondue with fresh strawberries, figs, sliced apples or pears, dried apricots, madeleines, or crunchy almond biscotti.

► *Makes about 2 cups; 6 to 8 servings*

1½ cups sweet dessert wine, such as orange muscat

1 tablespoon fresh lemon juice

1 teaspoon cornstarch

2 cups (1 pound) mascarpone cheese

1 In a medium nonreactive saucepan, boil the wine over high heat until it is reduced to about ⅔ cup, 10 to 12 minutes.

2 In a small bowl, stir the lemon juice with the cornstarch until completely blended. Whisk into the wine and return to a boil, stirring, until thickened and clear. Reduce the heat to low, gradually stir in the mascarpone, and cook until hot, 3 to 5 minutes.

3 Transfer to a ceramic fondue pot and set over a low flame. Regulate the heat, if possible, to keep the fondue warm, not hot.

DIPPING

sauces

ASIAN HERB SAUCE
with lime

Don't be intimidated by the list of ingredients. This zesty sauce is easily made in a food processor or blender. Although it keeps well in the refrigerator, the herbs will lose their fresh color over time. This sauce is ideal for chicken or seafood fondue.

► *Makes 1⅓ cups; 4 to 6 servings*

---

1 cup lightly packed fresh mint leaves

1 cup lightly packed fresh basil leaves

1 cup lightly packed fresh cilantro leaves

½ cup salted roasted cashews

3 tablespoons fresh lime juice

2 teaspoons finely grated fresh ginger

2 large garlic cloves, coarsely chopped

1½ teaspoons Asian fish sauce (*nam pla* or *nuoc nam*)

⅛ teaspoon freshly ground black pepper

1 cup vegetable oil

1 In a food processor or blender, combine the mint, basil, cilantro, cashews, lime juice, ginger, garlic, fish sauce, and pepper. Pulse until the ingredients are very finely chopped.

2 With the machine on, slowly pour in the oil until the sauce is well blended. Transfer to a small serving bowl and serve at once.

PONZU *dipping sauce*

This is a streamlined version of the tart Japanese dipping sauce often used with shabu-shabu. It also works perfectly well with any other meat, chicken, or seafood fondue. For a spicier sauce, add a coarsely chopped jalapeño pepper along with the ginger and shallot.

► *Makes about 1 cup; 4 to 6 servings*

⅓ cup soy sauce

¼ cup fresh lime juice

3 tablespoons fresh orange juice

2 tablespoons fresh lemon juice

1 tablespoon mirin (sweetened Japanese rice wine)

4 thin slices of fresh ginger, crushed with the flat side of a knife

1 small shallot, coarsely chopped

1 scallion, thinly sliced, for garnish

1 In a medium bowl, mix together the soy sauce, lime juice, orange juice, lemon juice, mirin, ginger, shallot, and 1½ tablespoons of water. Cover and refrigerate for at least 4 hours or overnight to blend the flavors.

2 Strain into a small serving bowl, pressing down gently on the solids with a rubber spatula to extract all of the liquid. Scatter the sliced scallion over the top and serve at once.

SESAME PEANUT *sauce*

Peanut sauce is equally suited for dipping skewered bits of cooked chicken, lamb, or beef, or any sort of crisp vegetable. This version is unique because it uses natural (unsweetened) peanut butter, requires no cooking, and contains a few unexpected ingredients that blend surprisingly well with the Asian flavors. For a richer, more unctuous sauce, replace the orange juice with canned unsweetened coconut milk.

► *Makes about 1⅓ cups; 4 to 6 servings*

½ cup natural peanut butter

¼ cup rice vinegar

3 tablespoons soy sauce

2 tablespoons Asian sesame oil

2 tablespoons orange juice

1 tablespoon honey

1 teaspoon finely grated fresh ginger

½ teaspoon Worcestershire sauce

½ teaspoon Dijon mustard

½ teaspoon Asian chili paste

1 In a medium bowl, combine the peanut butter, vinegar, soy sauce, sesame oil, orange juice, and honey. Stir until well blended. Stir in the ginger, Worcestershire, mustard, and chili paste.

2 Transfer the sauce to a small serving bowl. Serve at once, or cover and refrigerate for up to 8 hours. Let return to room temperature and stir well before serving.

CHIMICHURRI *sauce*

Chimichurri is a popular marinade and sauce in Argentina, where grilled beef is practically the national dish. Closer to home, this sauce is still irresistible with any meat or chicken fondue. Although *chimichurri* can be made well in advance, remember that the vinegar and lemon juice will eventually cause the parsley to discolor.

► *Makes 1¼ cups; 4 to 6 servings*

---

2 cups lightly packed flat-leaf parsley (about 1 large bunch)

¾ cup extra-virgin olive oil

¼ cup red wine vinegar

1 tablespoon fresh lemon juice

2 teaspoons dried oregano

3 garlic cloves, chopped

½ teaspoon salt

Dash of freshly ground black pepper

1 In a food processor or blender, combine the parsley, olive oil, vinegar, lemon juice, oregano, and garlic. Process until the ingredients are well blended and very finely chopped. Season with ½ teaspoon salt and a dash of pepper; then process again until almost smooth.

2 Transfer to a small serving bowl. Cover with plastic wrap and let the sauce stand at room temperature for up to 2 hours to allow the flavors to develop.

PIQUANT MINT *sauce*

Mint jelly used to be served with lamb, but this mint pesto is much more in keeping with contemporary tastes, and it also complements chicken and seafood cooked in the fondue pot. Fresh spearmint and peppermint are commonly available, but feel free to experiment with any other varieties you may have growing in your garden.

► *Makes 1½ cups; 4 to 6 servings*

---

3 cups packed fresh mint leaves

½ cup lightly packed flat-leaf parsley sprigs

⅓ cup cider vinegar

3 garlic cloves, coarsely chopped

1 medium shallot, coarsely chopped

½ cup mild olive oil or other vegetable oil

¼ teaspoon salt

Dash of freshly ground black pepper

1 In a food processor or blender, combine the mint, parsley, vinegar, garlic, and shallot. Pulse until the ingredients are very finely chopped.

2 With the machine on, slowly pour in the olive oil until blended. Season with the salt and pepper. Transfer to a small serving bowl and serve at once, or cover and let stand for up to 2 hours at room temperature to allow the flavors to develop.

SALSA VERDE

Italy's fresh herb sauce gets a big flavor-boost from anchovies, garlic, capers, and lemon. This version also includes bread crumbs for added body, to facilitate dipping. Virtually any meat or seafood fondue will benefit from these assertive yet perfectly balanced flavors.

► *Makes 1¼ cups*

---

2 cups packed flat-leaf parsley sprigs (about 1 large bunch)

⅔ cup extra-virgin olive oil

¼ cup *panko* (Japanese bread crumbs)

2 tablespoons drained capers plus 1 teaspoon of the brine

Finely grated zest and juice of 1 lemon

6 flat anchovy fillets packed in olive oil, drained

1 large garlic clove, coarsely chopped

⅛ teaspoon crushed hot red pepper

1 In a food processor or blender, combine the parsley, olive oil, *panko*, capers and caper brine, lemon zest, lemon juice, anchovies, garlic, and hot pepper flakes. Process until the ingredients are well blended and very finely chopped.

2 Transfer to a small serving bowl and serve at once, or cover and let stand for up to 1 hour at room temperature to allow the flavors to develop.

BÉARNAISE *mayonnaise*

Tarragon, white wine vinegar, and shallots are usually used to turn hollandaise sauce into sauce béarnaise. Here they create the same lush effect in a mayonnaise for dipping, that enhances beef, chicken, fish, and vegetables. Two forms of aromatic tarragon are used: the dried has the necessary intensity to infuse the wine reduction; and fresh tarragon adds the essential elegance to the finished sauce.

► *Makes about 1 cup; 4 servings*

⅓ cup dry white wine

⅓ cup white wine vinegar

¼ cup minced shallots

2 teaspoons dried tarragon

1 cup mayonnaise

1½ teaspoons Dijon mustard

1½ teaspoons fresh lemon juice

Freshly ground white pepper

1 tablespoon finely chopped fresh tarragon

1 In a small nonreactive saucepan, combine the wine, vinegar, shallots, and dried tarragon. Cook over medium heat, watching carefully, until the liquid is reduced to about 1 teaspoon. Scrape the reduction into a medium bowl and set aside to cool completely.

2 Add the mayonnaise, mustard, lemon juice, and a dash of pepper to the reduction. Blend well. Stir in the fresh tarragon. Transfer to a small serving bowl and serve at once, or cover and refrigerate for up to 4 hours.

CHIPOTLE *mayonnaise*

Chipotle chiles, which are smoked jalapeños, are sold dried or packed in adobo sauce in small cans. The canned variety is what's wanted here. Once opened, transfer the leftover chipotles and sauce to a jar with a tight-fitting lid and refrigerate. Stored this way, they will keep well for months.

► *Makes about 1 cup; 4 servings*

---

1 cup mayonnaise

1 tablespoon honey mustard

Finely grated zest and juice of 1 lime

1 garlic clove, crushed through a press

½ teaspoon ground cumin

½ teaspoon imported sweet paprika

2 canned chipotle chiles, with the adobo sauce that clings to them

1 In a medium bowl, combine the mayonnaise, mustard, lime zest, lime juice, garlic, cumin, and paprika. Whisk to blend well.

2 On a cutting board, use a large knife to mince the chipotles until they form a paste. Stir 2 teaspoons of the chipotle paste into the mayonnaise mixture. Cover and refrigerate for 1 hour to allow the flavors to develop. Taste and add the remaining chipotle paste if you'd like the sauce hotter. Transfer to a small serving bowl and serve at once, or refrigerate for up to 8 hours.

MADRAS CURRY *mayonnaise*

Black mustard seeds are available at Asian grocery stores and many well-stocked supermarkets. Although an optional ingredient for this sauce, they add an interesting element of texture and flavor. Do seek out Madras curry powder, as it is far more aromatic than most generic curry blends. Curry sauce is tremendously versatile, and particularly well suited for dipping vegetables, chicken, fish, and shellfish.

Makes about 1 cup; 4 servings

---

1 teaspoon black or brown mustard seeds (optional)

1 cup mayonnaise

1½ teaspoons Dijon mustard

1½ teaspoons Madras curry powder

¾ teaspoon ground cumin

½ teaspoon ground turmeric

¾ teaspoon finely grated fresh ginger

1 garlic clove, crushed through a press

Juice of 1 lime

Dash of cayenne pepper

1 If using the mustard seeds, toast them in a small dry skillet over medium heat, shaking the pan constantly so they don't burn, until the seeds are lightly toasted and fragrant, 30 seconds to 1 minute. (The seeds will start popping and jumping in the skillet.) Remove to a dish and set aside to cool completely.

2 In a medium bowl, whisk together the mayonnaise, mustard, curry powder, cumin, and turmeric. Stir in the ginger, garlic, lime juice, and a dash of cayenne. Stir in the reserved mustard seeds. Transfer the sauce to a small serving bowl. If you have time, cover and refrigerate for 2 hours to allow the flavors to develop.

SPICY ORANGE-GINGER *dipping sauce*

Adding just a few Asian pantry staples to ordinary mayonnaise transforms it into a fiery sauce with surprising depth of character. As versatile as it is delicious, try this sauce with vegetable, pork, beef, or shellfish fondue.

► *Makes 1¼ cups; 4 to 6 servings*

- 1 cup mayonnaise
- 4 teaspoons Asian sesame oil
- 1 tablespoon Dijon mustard
- 2 scallions, finely chopped
- 1 tablespoon finely grated fresh ginger
- Finely grated zest of 1 large orange
- 2 teaspoons soy sauce
- 2 teaspoons rice vinegar
- 1½ teaspoons Asian chili paste

1 In a medium bowl, whisk together the mayonnaise, sesame oil, and mustard until well blended. Stir in the scallions, ginger, orange zest, soy sauce, vinegar, and chili paste.

2 Transfer the sauce to a small serving bowl. Cover and refrigerate for 1 hour to allow the flavors to develop.

TANGY TARTAR *sauce*

Fried fish is incomplete without tartar sauce. This version travels uptown by using the tiny French sour gherkins known as cornichons. Look for them in gourmet shops and well-stocked supermarkets, packed in jars with a vinegar brine. Cornichons will keep almost indefinitely in the refrigerator.

► *Makes 1¼ cups; 4 to 6 servings*

---

1 cup mayonnaise

2 tablespoons white wine vinegar

1 tablespoon Dijon mustard

3 tablespoons finely chopped onion

2 tablespoons finely chopped cornichons (about 6 medium)

1 tablespoon drained tiny nonpareil capers

1 tablespoon chopped fresh parsley

1 tablespoon minced fresh chives

⅛ teaspoon freshly ground black pepper

1 In a medium bowl, mix together the mayonnaise, vinegar, and mustard. Add the onion, cornichons, capers, parsley, chives, and pepper. Mix until well blended.

2 Transfer the tartar sauce to a small serving bowl. If you have time, cover and refrigerate for at least 1 to 4 hours to allow the flavors to develop.

CREAMY HORSERADISH
sauce

This mildly pungent sauce packs plenty of flavor and comes together in a flash. It's a natural with beef fondue, but it also goes well with chicken and shrimp.

► *Makes 1¼ cups; 4 to 6 servings*

---

1 cup sour cream

¼ cup cream-style white horseradish

1 teaspoon fresh lemon juice

⅛ teaspoon salt

Dash of cayenne pepper

1 Combine the sour cream, horseradish, lemon juice, salt, and cayenne. Stir until well blended.

2 Transfer the sauce to a small serving bowl. Serve at once, or cover and refrigerate for up to 2 days.

SCANDINAVIAN MUSTARD *sauce*

No one can deny Scandinavians have a way with fish, so this sauce is a natural accompaniment for any of the seafood fondues. It also goes well with beef and pork.

► *Makes about 1 cup; 4 servings*

½ cup coarse country-style mustard

2 tablespoons sour cream

4 teaspoons light brown sugar

1 tablespoon cider vinegar

½ teaspoon ground allspice

Dash of salt

½ cup vegetable oil

1 In a medium bowl, whisk together the mustard, sour cream, sugar, vinegar, allspice, and salt. Gradually whisk in the oil until well blended.

2 Cover and refrigerate for at least 1 hour or up to a day in advance to allow the flavors to develop. Just before serving, whisk again to blend and transfer to a small serving bowl.

CUCUMBER-YOGURT *sauce with dill*

This refreshing combo makes an ideal dipping sauce for lamb, chicken, or vegetable fondue. English cucumbers are sometimes called hothouse cucumbers, and are sold protected in shrink-wrapped plastic. They are unwaxed, so they need no peeling.

► *Makes 2¾ cups; 6 to 8 servings*

---

1 small English (hothouse) cucumber, halved and seeded

2 cups plain Greek-style yogurt or other whole-milk yogurt, drained

2 tablespoons fresh lemon juice

1½ teaspoons Dijon mustard

1 garlic clove, crushed through a press

1 scallion, finely chopped

2 tablespoons finely chopped fresh dill or 2 teaspoons dried dill

¼ teaspoon salt

Dash of cayenne pepper

1 Shred the cucumber. Squeeze about one-third of the shredded cucumber in your hand to remove as much liquid as possible. Repeat with the remaining cucumber. There should be about 1¼ cups.

2 In a medium bowl, mix together the drained yogurt, lemon juice, mustard, and garlic. Stir in the cucumber, scallion, dill, salt, and cayenne. Transfer to a small serving bowl. Cover and refrigerate for up to 1 hour.

MINT-PESTO YOGURT

sauce

Garlic and mint are a natural with lamb, but this also makes a fine pairing with chicken or shellfish fondue. The pungent flavors of mint, garlic, and Parmesan are tamed and refreshed by the yogurt.

► *Makes about 1¾ cups; 6 to 8 servings*

⅓ cup pine nuts

2 garlic cloves, chopped

½ teaspoon salt

3 cups loosely packed fresh mint leaves

1 cup loosely packed flat-leaf parsley sprigs

¾ cup freshly grated Parmesan cheese

½ cup extra-virgin olive oil

1½ tablespoons fresh lemon juice

⅛ teaspoon freshly ground black pepper

6 tablespoons plain yogurt, preferably Greek-style

1 Place the pine nuts in a small dry skillet. Toast over medium-low heat, shaking the pan frequently, until the pine nuts are fragrant and lightly browned, 2 to 3 minutes. Transfer to a small dish and let cool.

2 In a food processor or blender, combine the garlic and salt. Process until the garlic is finely chopped. Add the pine nuts, mint, parsley, Parmesan, olive oil, lemon juice, and pepper. Process until a coarse paste forms.

3 Add the yogurt and mix just until blended. Transfer to a small serving bowl. Serve at once, or cover and refrigerate for up to 8 hours.

SPANISH ROASTED PEPPER *and hazelnut sauce*

Originating from Catalonia, the Spanish region that includes Barcelona, this sauce uses *pimentón,* a smoked Spanish paprika. If you can't find *pimentón,* use sweet paprika instead, and replace the hazelnuts with smoked almonds. The sauce was originally designed for seafood but has become a favored condiment for just about anything.

► *Makes 1½ cups; 6 servings*

¼ cup toasted skinned hazelnuts (filberts)

1 tablespoon *panko* (Japanese-style dry bread crumbs)

½ cup roasted red bell peppers, drained

½ cup drained canned fire-roasted or other diced tomatoes

2 tablespoons coarsely chopped onion

1 garlic clove, coarsely chopped

¾ teaspoon Spanish smoked paprika (*pimentón de la Vera*)

¼ teaspoon salt

Dash of cayenne pepper

¼ cup sherry vinegar or red wine vinegar

⅓ cup extra-virgin olive oil

1 Combine the hazelnuts and *panko* in a food processor. Pulse until the nuts are finely chopped. Add the roasted peppers, tomatoes, onion, garlic, smoked paprika, salt, and cayenne. Process until a coarse paste forms.

2 With the machine on, add the vinegar; then slowly add the oil in a thin stream until well blended. Transfer to a small serving bowl. Cover and let stand at room temperature for about 1 hour to allow the flavors to develop.

SEAFOOD COCKTAIL *sauce*

Fish and shellfish cooked in the fondue pot generally partner well with just about any ketchup-based dipping sauce. This one packs a little punch, softened by the cooling sensation of lime.

► *Makes about 1 cup*

---

1 cup ketchup

3 tablespoons prepared white horseradish

1 tablespoon Worcestershire sauce

Finely grated zest and juice of 1 lime

1 small garlic clove, crushed through a press

1 small shallot, minced

½ teaspoon hot pepper sauce

1 In a medium bowl, combine the ketchup, horseradish, Worcestershire, lime zest, lime juice, garlic, shallot, and hot sauce. Stir until well blended.

2 Transfer the sauce to a small serving bowl. Cover and refrigerate for at least 1 hour to allow the flavors to develop.

ZESTY ASIAN-STYLE *cocktail sauce*

While this intensely flavored dipping sauce stands up well to beef or pork cooked in the fondue pot, it also makes a tasty condiment for poached or fried shellfish, such as scallops and prawns, and batter-fried vegetables like zucchini and artichoke hearts.

► *Makes about 1¼ cups; 4 to 6 servings*

---

1 cup ketchup

2 tablespoons mirin (sweetened Japanese rice wine)

2 tablespoons soy sauce

2 teaspoons Asian sesame oil

1½ tablespoons finely chopped cilantro

1 tablespoon minced garlic

1 In a medium bowl, combine the ketchup, mirin, soy sauce, Asian sesame oil, cilantro, and garlic. Stir until well blended.

2 Transfer the sauce to a small serving bowl. Cover and refrigerate for about 1 hour to allow the flavors to develop.

PUTTANESCA *dipping sauce*

This classic Italian sauce is named for the, um, ladies of the red-light district, because—like them—it's spicy and quickly made. Serve with chicken, beef, or vegetable fondues, and especially with Fried Tortelloni Fondue (page 58).

► *Makes about 2 cups; 6 to 8 servings*

---

1 can (14½ ounces) crushed tomatoes

½ cup pitted Kalamata olives, coarsely chopped

1 tin (2 ounces) flat anchovy fillets, drained and chopped

2 tablespoons drained tiny nonpareil capers

1 tablespoon extra-virgin olive oil

2 garlic cloves, minced

⅛ teaspoon crushed hot red pepper

¼ cup chopped flat-leaf parsley

1 In a small nonreactive saucepan, combine the tomatoes, olives, anchovies, capers, olive oil, garlic, and hot pepper flakes. Cook over medium heat, stirring occasionally, for about 10 minutes, until the flavors have blended and the mixture has thickened slightly.

2 Stir in the parsley. Transfer to a medium bowl and serve warm or at room temperature.

INDEX